PIGTAILS AND OTHER TALES

Growing up in Indian Cove in the '50s and '60s

With Recipes to Taste It

MAXINE HOOLEY PEIRSON

DITCH RIDER PUBLISHING

Max, Maxie, Mackie, Maxine grew up with all the other children of the fifties and sixties, beginning at the end of that first year, 1950. What is unique for her is being a Hooley and growing up in Indian Cove. She left home for a high school diploma from Western Mennonite High School in Salem, Oregon, followed by college, a career, college, children, college, and a second career in teaching. Interspersed throughout these things have been retreats back to the Cove, for family times, to swing a hoe in the sugar beets, ride the potato digger, pick vegetables from the garden or raspberries from the berry patch, run down a nearby dune, and in many ways enjoy the tasks and the tastes of home and family in that blessed valley.

ISBN 978-1548231859

Edited by Anne J. Stanton, Joanna Ortega
Illustrations by Sarah Hooley
Cover design & LaTeX layout by Nathaniel D. Peirson
Cover photographs provided by author
Front: Doris and Wes Hooley with their five eldest children
Back: Hooley children with Kauffman cousins
Cover image by Christian Salwa, used under CC0
Fonts and packages used in accordance with Apache 2.0

www.ditchwriter.com
DITCH RIDER PUBLISHING

for the hardworking farmers
their hardworking wives
and their hardworking children

The Cove is Indian Cove, a valley held between the Snake River, the rimrocks, and the sandy Owyhee desert to the south. And the Cove is the folks of this valley and how they have held in place a livelihood and a community by drawing from this river and from the individuality and faith of each other. The stories of growing up in the Cove are sent out for remembering, and for the stirring up and telling of more stories from those who also grew up there.

In telling our Cove stories, we can all look back and marvel at its beginnings, the hardships and the hard work of all who came before us—those true pioneers. Daddy says that what got him through the grueling hard work back in the forties, as they hand-dug their well, leveled dunes, and carved out courses to take the water to fields and crop rows, was the anticipation. May all of us be so blessed with strong anticipation for the tasks we have before us. We have them to thank for this.

Introduction

Long ago, in a far away land nestled among towering rimrocks, a small group of people struggled to become a community. In the dawn of my memory, I can see these resilient dreamers toiling to bring farms to life from the isolated sandy desert. Fighting dust storms, scorching heat, and harsh winters, they carved a livelihood from the soil where sagebrush and sand dunes once stood. For you see, the strong moody river quietly moving through this valley is willing to give it life if you have the tenacity to channel water to the land.

Listen to the stories from the heart of this pioneer daughter who gives glimpses of the voices echoing from the past. These voices speak of the dream of an idyllic life: fearing God, loving one's neighbor, doing one's best under the elusive watchful eye of the wild cat and circling birds of prey.

Foreword by Gary Hooley, who has many more Cove stories to share.

TABLE OF

CONTENTS

Maxine Faye Hooley

Chapter 1

Sandbox World

A CHILD'S BEST WORLD has holding places, large and small, for growing and playing, all safe and secure. Indian Cove is a valley cradled by rimrocks and a river, and our place sits on the west end of this cove. The lanes in the valley didn't have names back then, but were simply roads off of Highway 78, the county highway that crosses the top side of Owyhee County. Our house sits on the gravel road that also led folks to Willards, to Miltons, to Shenks, to Rippes, to Hamiltons, and to Bob Goods, and then goes on down into the canyon of the Snake River. The river supplied our irrigation water, and fishing and swimming holes, along with grazing for a small herd of cattle. If a car went by that we didn't recognize, well, it was probably someone from out of our valley heading down to a fishing hole.

The third house down the lane was our house; the home of Wes and Doris Hooley, and their family that would become nine. Daddy had added on rooms as we grew, and sided it with green shingles. He laid down varnished plywood atop our little table so it could always hold all of us for eating our three square meals a day, together.

Outside across the drive from the house sat our sandbox on the edge of the green grassy cow pasture and chicken yard, squarely under the shade of the maple tree. This big tree sported a board swing. For a little while, my brother Dale had one of his many tree houses perched overhead. The sandbox was our world-in-the-making, where we mirrored our own Cove with its fields, its homes with yards and gardens, and its lanes leading here and there across its countryside. The sandbox was a safe, child-size slice of life as we knew it.

In a sandbox, the sand must first be cleared of 'cat logs' to prepare it for homesteading. Acreages were platted out according to the number of us playing there that day. Red bricks made simple houses, or homes could be built using wet sand molded into shape. Yards were landscaped with various leafy plant tips. From "Indian Tobacco," which grew tall heads of colorful seeds, green to red, on the nearby ditch bank, we stripped off handfuls to spread for yards or gardens, planted row by row. And the Spirea bush tips were perfect for our plantings, with their tiny clustered leaves. Our fields were outlined using the tip of a stick, and were bordered with twig fence rows. A classier fence could be built using forked elm twigs and straight little pieces laid out between them, like a log fence Abe Lincoln used to make. Over the farmscape, the roads from 'my place to your place' were rolled out by tin cans.

When the pasture around us was flood-irrigated,

a small hole was opened on a side board of the sand-box to allow a little water in to make its way down our carefully made ditches. We tried to coax the water into miniature corrugates created by press-ing the tines of a piece of an old square-meshed laundry basket across the sand fields. Great care was taken to manage the water to avoid flooding, a job particularly engaging for my brothers, all three who were to become farmers 'for real.'

Sometimes our world expanded outside of the sandbox to include the nearby irrigation ditch. When empty, its damp sides were excavated for ascending and descending roads, and a nearby town emerged in its valley. Mounted old radio tubes became an electric power plant. Matchbox cars came in the sixties, to traffic between that ditch town and the sandbox countryside.

It was Mama who took me out to play in the empty ditch that first time. It was still wet from recently irrigating the garden. The water always carries sand and drops some along the way, leaving ditch bottoms almost as good as a sandbox, when not in use. She stooped down and packed sand around my foot, patting a roof shape on top and nice straight sides. Then she helped me to pull out my foot, slowly and carefully. Using both hands she packed on a front wall to my marvelous little house, and a stick carefully opened up a doorway and a window. This was the best kind of house a sandbox child could want: a house that is waiting for its yard and garden, its fence rows and fields, and its neighbors. "Let's stretch out a road, now, so I can come to your house, and you can come to mine!"

Of course, our sandbox was good for more than country landscapes. Wet sand is a sculptor's medium. One day, we had a wedding, and a large sand cake was shaped on a board; elegantly decorated with roses and garden flowers. We carefully carried it across the drive to the front lawn. This really must have been some wedding, because the family photo album holds a picture of it. It shows a bride garbed in a gauzy white curtain gown and veil, a groom dressed up in his father's real suit, and a coerced three-year old preacher looking quite official in the black sweater we had put on him backwards, a Bible in his hands.

Some things take children out of their sandbox in the summertime besides dinner and the dusk of evening. As we grew older, there were more farm tasks for us to do. The boys began to drive tractors, and the girls sometimes, too. Judy was depended on in the kitchen, and haying took a steady crew to craft lofty haystacks. The garden's harvest of peas, beans, cukes, corn, red beets, and tomatoes needed willing hands because there were freezer boxes and canning jars to fill, expeditiously, as each vegetable and fruit came on in its time.

> *Giant sun-baked loaf*
> *Children fork alfalfa hay*
> *from Farmhand mouthfuls*

And so there was less and less time spent in the sandbox. Maybe it was jealousy that prompted Dale to tease a sandbox-contented younger brother into touching the electric fence around the pasture with "see...it's not hot," until, of course, it was reconnected to the hot wire the instant the trusting hand reached out to wrap around the live wire. Since the sandbox sat inside the pasture, fenced to keep the milk cow, we knew to duck under that electric wire for our comings and goings.

The Cove world—both inside and outside of our sandbox—contained contentment a'plenty for our growing up. Although the sandbox disappeared after we no longer played in it, that green friendly house still holds us, whenever we can get there to be together.

Sandbox World

Recipes for Children

Sunshine Tea for Dolls

Gather the lilac leaves from the nearby bushes. Place leaves in a little tea pot or a pan filled with water. Let it steep outside in the sun beside the playhouse, until the color is just right for tea. Enjoy with mud cakes, also prepared in the sun.

Eskimo Cookies

This recipe comes from a colorful little cookbook Judy received when she was young and the rest of us were younger still.

½ stick margarine or butter, softened and well beaten
¾ cup sugar
1 T. water
½ tsp. vanilla
3 T. cocoa
2 cups oatmeal

Blend butter and sugar. Mix in the water, vanilla, and cocoa. Add the oatmeal and mix well. Refrigerate. Then shape dough into 26 balls, and place onto waxed paper. Roll them in powdered sugar. Now that they are white like Eskimo children in polar bear parkas, they are ready to eat.

Sherbet

Hot days in Summer need cool refreshing desserts. I could expect to hear Daddy calling, when he served ice cream around four o'clock, "Ice cream, you scream; We all scream, but Maxine!" I preferred Mama's cool refreshing fruit "sherberts" over store-bought ice cream.

1 large box of Jello from storage under the bed
Sugar, to taste
3–4 cups milk from the Jersey cow or Amos' dairy truck

Mix jello and sugar with ¼ cup hot water to dissolve. Pour into an ice cube tray or baking dish. Place in freezer. When frozen, break it up into the blender and whirl with milk. Pour back into the container to re-freeze.

Chapter 2

Days of Our Lives

THE DAYS of our lives in the Cove revolved around three square meals a day. We grew up with breakfast, dinner and supper, each set before us at the family table; a table laid out from God's bounty, by hand, and from scratch.

It is time to come to the table when Daddy has reached the end of a corrugate or a field, near meal time, and has come in to wash up. Mama's holler, "Children, come to the table, now!" gets us going, too. There we are, seated around the table in our usual places, with Daddy at the end and Mama on his left next to the kitchen, and with littler ones between us older ones all around the table. We sing grace:

> Thank you for the world so sweet.
> Thank you for the food we eat.
> Thank you for the birds that sing,
> Thank you, God, for everything. Amen.

In springtime, the first dandelions come to the table wilted by the hot bacon dressing Mama drizzles over them, and chubby spears of asparagus are served up from ditch banks. Come summertime, we march dinner fresh from the garden to the table in not much more than an hour before serving it, all washed, sliced, diced, cooked up, and poured into the colorful serving bowls. Throughout the year, food can be brought up from the cellar's canning shelves and from the big green chest freezer in the cabin, where it had all been 'put up' properly as each had come on for harvest. There are daily chicken layers, the milk cow, weekly baking days, and seasonal butchering days. The Hammett grocery store is nine miles down the road, and Amos' dairy delivery truck passes by our house on his way home each day. This is how all of the necessaries come through Mama's hardworking hands to feed her family, just so.

"Pass the chicken, please." There is a piece for each of us: some like dark meat and some like light, and Mama has convinced us she prefers the neck. It is my privilege to claim the organ meats; the heart, the liver and that chewy gizzard. Then the spuds (potatoes) and other vegetables are passed around with the pickles, the bread, and the butter and jam all following. Lastly, the jewel-colored fruits appear—peaches, apricots, cherries, pears, or prunes—spooned from Kerr or Mason jars to join cookies or cake, if not pie.

Our chatter passes around the family table, too. Some like to listen, and some like to talk. We sit between Daddy, deep in quiet thought, and Mama watching for who might be needing something more on their plate. How unthinkable, I muse, that in the 'olden days,' children were to be seen and not heard, for we are some of both. What Daddy and

Mama want to see and hear is common ordinary table manners, our plates scraped clean, and any talk of other folks spoken in only the kindest of ways. Some are unspoken rules that we have, and some are clearly stated:

"Don't say it, if it isn't nice."

"*Kids* means baby goats, so say *children,* please."

And then come the dishes—always the dishes! "It's your turn," is quickly pointed out to the one with the clearly counted turn.

"No, it's not; I did them last time!" But, alas, the turn sticks fast. What an interminable process it is to wash the dishes, with a wet stomach to show for it and less time to play. Mama says girls in 'her day' were told that getting a wet dress from doing the dishes meant they would marry a drunkard! I sigh, knowing a wet front is unavoidable, for me, though I know of no drinking man in our valley.

One day, Daddy says to me, "Let me show you how to wash the dishes." He puts all the glasses in the warm soapy water first, and then the silverware to the right. Next come the plates, all nicely stacked up, then serving bowls, and lastly the pans to be scrubbed.

"Look, I'm done, and the water is still sudsy and warm!" After this demonstration of a niftily organized sink, this chore is never quite the same for me again. Now I could forever be a contented dishwasher, ready to swap out dishes for some other unwanted task!

When a grocery list becomes sufficiently neces-sary, it is time for a trip to Hammett store. Mama's list keeps us stocked in flour, sugar, Jello, soap, shortening, often bananas, oranges in winter, toilet paper, rice, macaroni, and packets of Kool-Aid in the summer. First, the grocers are the "Hineys," and then the "Harmons." When "Hineys," it is always our chance to snicker; since a 'hiney' to us is our own behinds. Mr. Harmon is a generous man who lets Daddy charge our stock-up on groceries, which is a very good thing since money only comes to the farm after the fall harvest. Buying in bulk creates makeshift pantries under our beds: "You got Jello under your bed?" This is far better than space for the boogey man, we think to ourselves!

For us, the grocers' is more than Mama's list. With pennies in hand we eye the candy shelf with its tootsie rolls, sweet tarts, bubble gum, malt balls, licorice, and lollipops; all penny candy there for our choosing.

When my big sister is bussed out of Hammett to the King Hill Junior High, it becomes my task after school to walk the catty-corner path to the tiny post office for our mail. There I turn the little brass dial on Box #72, pointing it to the secret combination numbers all in right order, to open the postal box. Next, on to the grocery store with coins for my usual tootsie roll, and then the walk back to school through the park. This after-school route is best with the Waller twins, walking arm in arm in arm, with me in the middle of them, bubbling along like life could get no better!

It is on this catty-corner path on the after-school walk that I am offered my first bottle of pop. When I tip it to my lips, I discover that sweet fizzy tingle and burp that rushes up on an unsuspecting nose.

"Oh, why didn't someone tell me?!" I yelp inside. I dare not say anything aloud, feeling clueless and not wanting anyone to know I had never drunk pop before. This is a first time I sheepishly choose silence for the want of fitting in, hiding from that nasty little secret that maybe, just maybe, I might be different from other children in ways I wouldn't wish to be.

Then it is time to board the bus for the ride back into the Cove for home. There in the valley our family lives, sitting together at our table, singing the always thankful prayer before our always tasty meals, and the dishes always following along, afterwards. I remember these well-ordered days of our lives.

When my big sister Judy brings home a plaque to hang above the table, it gives us pause on what we have been doing—at least, it does for me. "It won't always be like this," I think, as much as it seems like an 'always' kind of thing. The plaque remains hanging above that kitchen table. It reads:

BLESS OUR HOME
Father that we
Cherish the bread
Before there is none,
Discover each other
Before we leave,
And enjoy each
Other for what
We are while
We have time.

By Richard Wong

Recipes from our Everyday Table

Wilted Dandelion Salad

With spring came fresh greens; a welcome taste after passing through winter without them. Dandelions appear in the grass, and asparagus is picked off the ditch banks—Dave's ditches down the road, by his invitation.

Toss spring-fresh dandelion leaves with this warm dressing before serving:

Bacon Dressing
4 slices of bacon, fried crispy and broken up
1 T. vinegar
1½ T. sugar

Asparagus on Toast

Covering spears of asparagus with a cheesy warm sauce on toast makes them delectably palatable for children. This may have been Grandma Yoder's way of doing things, which Daddy then showed to Mama.

Asparagus
Salt to taste
4–6 slices of bread, toasted
Cheese, grated

Snap off and throw away the woody parts of the

asparagus spears. Wash and steam in a little water until fork-tender. Drain and keep warm. Prepare boiled eggs, peel and slice into rounds.

Make a white sauce by mixing flour with butter melted in a little saucepan. Slowly add milk and a little salt, stirring until it thickens.

Toast slices of bread and butter them. Cut into halves. Place a row of asparagus spears across each piece of toast. Spoon hot white sauce across them. Slice eggs and arrange across the mounds. Grate cheese and sprinkle on each serving. Broil to melt the cheese.

Homemade Bread

Homemade bread was most basic to our three square meals, in all seasons. Mama's bread recipe didn't stay exactly the same over the years. She would reduce the oil in the 'less is best' trend for oils, and she came to add some whole wheat to the white, and a little oats. One thing that did stay the same, however, was the moist deliciousness of her fresh bread! This is her recipe that I came to use for making bread for my own family.

2¼ cups water
1½ T. yeast
¼ cup brown sugar
1 T. salt
½ cup oats
1½–2 cups whole wheat flour
1½ T. oil
2½–3 cups unbleached flour
    (or Better for Bread flour)

Let the yeast dissolve and fluff-up the water. Add the sugar, salt, oats, whole wheat flour, and oil. Mix well. Work in enough bread flour to make a firm dough. Knead at least ten minutes. Let it rise, punch it down, and let it rise again. Form into two loaves and place into greased bread pans.

When fully risen, preheat oven to 425 °F.
Bake for 20–25 minutes. You can tell if it is done by snipping the tops, listening for a lighter sound.

Chapter 3

A Taste of the Far Side

IN THE QUIET EBB AND FLOW of everyday life in the Cove, everything usually went along as it should. There, the farmer and his wife, with the children under their orchestration, managed everything in concert with nature's own daily and seasonal rhythms.

What I didn't know until I grew up and had it pointed out to me by cartoonist Gary Larson[1] is that there are simultaneous universes spinning on the farm. There was our farm family going on about its farm life, and there were the cows in their reality, busy with their bovine lives. When I say they were busy, I mean the cows were probably grazing, swatting flies with their tails, or lazily chewing their cud. One day, like a bolt of lightning, these two worlds collided on the Hooley farm.

I had rabbits at the time, all hutched up next to the chicken house inside the cow pasture. They needed fresh alfalfa, and, being a whole warren of

---

[1] Gary Larson is an American cartoonist and the creator of *The Far Side*, printing in newspapers from 1985 to 1990.

rabbits, would require a tubful to do the job. I had no clue that a couple of white, pretty, pink-eyed rabbits would become two dozen in just a few months. They were beyond my control, and I needed help to manage things! Mama knew I could not carry a big wash tub full of alfalfa by myself, so she compelled my sister Donna to stop what she was happily doing, to help me gather the fresh feed. Terribly put out with me for this imposition, she proceeded to 'show' me, by forcing us into a chasm of silence while we did the job. We set to work without summertime chatter, without congenial conversation, without a single bickering banter; with only an intolerably cold silence between us. I cut handfuls of alfalfa as rapidly as I could to end the tortuous sentence of her mean grip, for to ban me from dialogue was to imprison my very soul.

When the tub was full, Donna and I carried it between us out of the field and across the barnyard. At the pasture fence, we hoisted it up to the top rail, balancing it as we clambered over. Poised there atop the fence, the aroma of fresh-cut alfalfa hay wafted through the quiet summer air. Suddenly, our Jersey cow came shooting out from behind the nearby milking shed. Her lolliping udder and ecstatic moos careened right toward us! We must have been way too quiet to be seen, and she had her eyes on that heaped up tub—a bountiful bowlful of succulent summer salad. We could not have been more surprised had she stood on her two hind legs, napkin and fork poised, ready for us to serve up her lunch!

Faster than bullets we flew under and through

the fence rails, the tub landing in the pasture in front of the eager cow. As we tumbled to the ground, our words and laughter were shaken loose from our tight-lidded lips like marbles spilling from an opened bag! Gone in an instant were those painfully mute moments: we were, once again, two lively sisters enjoying the day together.

What I suspect is that wherever there is an available cow or two, nature stands ready to give a jolt, just to see children get their bounce back. Congenial sisters are as crucial to the whole farm as sunshine. Just as in *The Far Side*, cows can be very good at this sort of thing. I am quite certain that our Jersey cow enjoyed this bump in time, kicking up her heels for lunch that day, on us.

Recipes from the Barnyard

Fried Rabbit

A couple of rabbits on the farm can make perfect pets, but when they become too numerous, they might show up on the dinner table, tasting much like chicken. Fried rabbit is so good that it needs no special treatment to prepare and serve.

1 Rabbit, skinned and cut up for frying
Flour
Shortening
Salt and pepper to taste

Simply dust pieces with flour, sprinkle with salt and pepper, and fry in melted shortening to a golden crispy perfection.

Homemade Butter

Like a platter of Rocky Mountain Oysters,[2] rabbit is not likely to appear—magically or otherwise—on your dinner table. Instead, you might consider making butter from a Jersey cow's rich cream.

Skim off the cream from the top of milk, and pour it into a blender. Whirl until the milk separates

[2]Rocky Mountain Oysters is a dish made of fried bull, pig, or sheep testicles. We didn't eat them, but heard that the Basque sheepherders did.

from the cream, and chunky yellow blobs appear in buttermilk. Pour into a bowl. Fish out all the blobs with your fingers, pushing them together into one large soft one. Holding your hands under a trickle of cold water, gently work the butter to remove the pockets of buttermilk. Sprinkle with salt, and work it in. Shape your butter into a satisfying cube or mound. Refrigerate to keep butter firm.

Angel Food Cake

Our diets have changed somewhat over time, with our boxed mixes and microwave cooking. The local supermarkets now bring to us fresh fruits and vegetables year 'round. Here are two recipes that don't need to change with the times.

A birthday in the family is worth the effort of making a cake from scratch—like the chickens do— spread generously with shiny Seven Minute Icing.

1¼ cups egg whites, room temperature
¼ tsp. salt
1¼ tsp. cream of tartar
1 tsp. vanilla
¼ tsp. almond extract
1 cup cake flour
1½ cups sugar

Preheat oven to 375 °F.

Whip egg whites with salt and cream of tartar at high speed until stiff peaks form. Do not under beat! Beat in the vanilla and almond extract. Sift the flour and sugar together several times. Fold them into the egg whites. Pour into a tube pan. Cut through it with a knife in several places to get rid of air pockets.

Bake 30 minutes at 375 °F, or until it is a dry, golden brown. Remove from the oven and invert. (Use a pop bottle, or something akin to it, to avoid touching the top of the cake to the plate.)

Seven-Minute Icing

This recipe is enough icing for two 8-inch layers, or one Angel Food cake.

1 egg white
⅛ tsp. cream of tartar
3 T. cold water
¾ cup sugar
½ tsp. vanilla

Put everything—except vanilla—together into a double boiler. Place over rapidly boiling water. Beat until it's stiff enough to stand up in peaks (about seven minutes for a hand beater and four minutes with an electric mixer). If it has a grainy appearance, add a few drops of lemon juice and beat until smooth. Mix in the vanilla. Frost the cake immediately, before the surface of the icing turns crispy. This icing shows colors brilliantly when food coloring is added.

Chapter 4

Going to the Fourth of July

IN INDIAN COVE, the farming valley was quilted neatly with fields, and the world turned on the routines of daily life, pausing momentarily each week for a Sunday or a Sabbath rest, and riding on the swells of the weeks and the rotating seasons as each came with its own 'to-do' lists and get-togethers. Family life and the community were in sync with nature's rhythms, as well as the calendar for school days. As each holiday came, it was kept in our own customary ways.

One holiday that stood out almost as tall as Christmas was the single day of each summer when everyone in the valley put down their shovels and hoes and "went to the Fourth of July." Prepared with picnic blankets, potluck dishes, and excited children, the cars and pickups headed down the road that curved along the Snake River, bridged over it, rolled us through Hammett, and then took us north across the desert and up into the foothills of the Rocky Mountains. Here, lupines painted the outlines of the roads lavender, and sunflower polka dots scattered over the hillsides. Dad would stop the white chubby 1949 Mercury, and we children could finally shake the kinks out of our car-cramped legs by tumbling out and scattering among the tall yellow heads for a Kodak photograph.

Bennett Mountain sits on top of the foothills where sagebrush meets birch trees, grassy meadows, and blooming Syringa. Here, pine trees march up its steep sides to the brushy, rocky top. It belonged to the sheep rancher of Hammett whose wintering pens patchworked the east end of our valley. His Basque sheepherders wintered, there, in a communal bunkhouse there, and, come spring, after lambing and sheering, they headed out with the flocks to these higher grazing grounds. We would hope to spot a white canvas-topped wagon with a man and his sheep dog somewhere along the way, and wonder how the sheepherder could live so lonely up there, alone. But Bennett Mountain itself was ours for the day, when we "went to the Fourth of July."

"Are we almost there yet?" we children would ask when we'd had quite enough of the going, and then fall silent with anticipation as our car turned onto a dusty, two-track lane. The way opened and all of the arriving vehicles arranged themselves there, on the grass, spilling out this family, that family, and all of the other families from the Cove.

Dave Shenk would already be there, hat on and smiling, sitting cross-legged, his arms also crossed and dangling over his top leg. He was our neighbor who lived alone down the road from us and provided long, thought-out prophetic sketches of the end-times to come, for those who dropped by his simple home. He would have been one of the first to arrive at the Fourth of July picnic in his classy Frazier, because he made the coffee. We were never early enough to see how the little old wood stove came to be under the tree, but there it stood with a tall urn of coffee atop it, hot, percolated, and ready for each stout "ahh," and the growing conviviality.

Large plywood boards straddled wooden sawhorses under a group of shady trees and quickly became a mix of flowered and checkered tablecloths all collaged with covered bowls and pans. Towels wrapped tightly around the hot dishes so the smells would not come out until everyone was ready.

But children don't wait for food. They take off to explore, eagerly moving beyond the picnic spread to a bubbling, fresh, foot-numbingly cold creek with a log over it for crossing to the other side. There, the mountain rises steeply, ready for our fun: climbing up, running down, dodging trees, and doing it all over again. The mountain would soon wear a delightfully dusty hem, there by the creek where we braked to our stops.

Before children get very dirty or the deviled eggs and potato salads can grow Salmonella, everyone circles in closely and becomes very still to catch the pastor's prayer as it spreads blessings over all the food, over all of us, and then over the creek; up and over Bennett mountain, out beyond the spacious skies, the waving grain; the whole great country of majestic mountains, fruitful plains, and the valleys, including our own Cove below. Then, we all join in four-part harmony to send the Doxology to the top of the trees, to the top of that great blue sky, and to God. We sing:

Praise God from whom all blessings flow.
Praise Him all creatures here below.
Praise Him above Ye heavenly hosts.
Praise Father, Son, and Holy Ghost. Amen.

Our community potlucks could be counted on for fried chicken, deviled eggs, potatoes in salads or scalloped, all the other salads, pickles, fresh-baked rolls, cookies, pies, and cakes. A potluck can offer new surprises, too. *What are those odd, gnarly, tasteless balls hiding in Almeda's bean salad!* And when desserts are laid out, I spy toasted coconut icing atop the oatmeal cake that Fan's sister from Filer brought.

At last, the women folk can cluster together for precious visiting time, while the men fling their horse shoes, or crack bats and catch flies with the boys, in the clearing. The giggling teenage girls search for the pop hidden by the boys somewhere in the creek. The children are breathless from hiking, running, and chasing flitting Swallowtail butterflies.

No flags were unfurled when we went to the Fourth of July each year, and I don't remember hearing any patriotic speeches. But we knew with a young and deep knowing that freedom had everything to do with all the valley folks relaxing together in afternoon contentment on Bennett Mountain.

When the time comes to head home for irrigating and milking, all bare feet must skid to a halt at the edge of the creek, to be cleaned off in its cold water. Then, for our grand finale, Amos Shenk would pull out the tall, green canvas-covered canister from his weekday Darigold delivery truck, and generously scoop refreshing ice cream, placing a cone into each and every hand. Goodbyes are passed all around.

Finally, dusty, tired children are collected into cars ready to take them back home to the Cove; back down into the valley's gentle and steadily turning world. In our car, I suspect Daddy and Mama were tired, too, but still they would smile when they heard us asking, "When do we get to go back to the Fourth of July?"

Recipes from Potlucks & Picnics

The recipes we hang onto and still use years later are akin to leafing through a photo album. And the tastes and smells triggered by memories of summer air and a community picnic bring back heaps of keen remembering!

Red Beet Pickles
From the Kerr Home Canning Book

Select small, young beets, cook until tender, dip into cold water. Peel off skins. Make the following syrup:

2 cups sugar
2 cups water
2 cups strong vinegar (4-6% acidity)
1 tsp. cloves
1 tsp. allspice
1 T. cinnamon

Pour over beets and boil 10 minutes. Pack into sterilized Kerr jars and seal.

Helen Johnson's Mustard Pickles

6 quarts cucumbers, peeled and cubed, and soaked
    in one cup of salt water for two hours, then
    drained.
2 quarts onions, sliced thinly
2 cups sugar
1½ quarts vinegar
2 T. dry mustard
1 tsp. tumeric

Mix together the cukes and other ingredients. Use
fresh, or pack in jars to can. To can, process the
jars according to Kerr canning methods.

Oatmeal Cake
(Esther's cake)

1¼ cups boiling water
1¼ cups quick oats
1 stick of butter

Pour boiling water over oats, and add butter.

Let stand 20 minutes, then add:

1 cup white sugar
1 cup brown sugar
2 tsp. vanilla
1 ⅔ cups flour
1 tsp. salt
1 tsp. soda
1 tsp. cinnamon
2 eggs

Beat all together. Bake 30 minutes at 375 °F. Prepare icing recipe below.

Oatmeal Cake Toasted Icing

6 T. butter
¼ cup cream
1 cup shredded coconut
1 cup white sugar

Mix, and pour over the cake. Toast lightly.

Chapter 5

Custom-Made Cousins

THE WATKINS MAN and the Sears Roebuck catalog brought farm families the chance to get what couldn't be had from field, barnyard, sewing machine, or a drive out of our Cove valley. Both of these came to our door each year. The tall bottle of vanilla and our big can of pepper we bought from the Watkins Man, and Mama catalog-ordered our bed sheets, towels, socks, underwear, and the jeans for Daddy and the boys. Mama recalled using pages from the Monkey Wards (Montgomery Wards) catalog crumpled soft for toilet paper in the outhouse when she was a girl. We children only knew the catalogs for their appealing pictures of wonderful things that might be had by mail-order. However, one of the essentials for growing up that we did not need to send away for, was cousins. We had our own custom-made Kauffman cousins.

Auntie Norma and Uncle Vernon grew a whole family of fun cousins over at their place across the fields, and they spaced them both above and beside us in age so that we would have some to look up to, and some smack-dab our sizes. They were farm-grown and beautiful: Carol, Eileen, Karen, Betty, and then Vesta, who was my age. The brothers were handsome and inventive: Pete, Arden, Kenneth, Howard and Wilbur, although Pete and Arden were pretty much grown up and gone before I knew them. Our Kauffman cousins entranced us, and their quick wit often left me behind trying to catch up. Their drama and play engaged us in ways we did not dream up on our own! And they laughed a lot. I figured that laughter in a family comes in proportion to its size.

I have a tiny cousin memory of Karen taking care of us, probably when Mama went to have another baby, since that would have been the only reason for having a "babysitter" in those days. The stories Karen wove for us were incredible tales of mice in enchanting labyrinthian lands and cozy hole homes. And there is the memory of sleeping out my fevered days with German measles in a darkened room at the Kauffmans. Mama did everything she could to contain viruses when they showed up at our house because my sister's and brothers' kidneys kept an exacting score of any and all infections. I guess the Kauffmans had all run through the measles—which must have been quite a feat—and could spare a sick room for me.

Now, farm families are very busy. They are so busy, in fact, that they can't get together as much as they would like to. When Auntie Norma drove over with some of her children to see my Mama, they couldn't get all their visiting squeezed in before it was time for them to get back home for milking. So they kept chatting together as she eased her car back out the driveway, with me—known as "Mackie" only to her—standing on the running board, hoping and hoping they had yet one more thing to say before she reached the road.

The Kauffman girls were very fashionable, and they cooked gourmet long before I'd heard that word, sprinkling herbs on their everyday green beans. The boys had mysterious card games with kings, queens, and jack faces, hidden under their beds in the basement. Outside, they created cars for driving that were imaginary except for stick steering wheels, or they used shovels to carve out vehicles into the ground, back in the tree row, with dirt humps sculpted for seats and real steering wheels sticking out from earthen dashboards.

And there were the games, games, and more games we played together: *Red Rover Red Rover, Red Light Green Light, Annie-I-Over, Mother May I,* and *Kick the Can.* I learned the hard way to do my running through the hand-holds of younger players in *Red Rover,* rather than trying to blast through the chest-high immovable barricade Ken and Howard held firmly in place, which would knock me flat on my back.

Vesta was my very best playmate. She teased me when I misread "manure" as "manyur," but we were still closest of cousins. While her big sisters turned out their fashions on the sewing machine, we were contentedly cutting ours out of the Sears Roebuck catalogs. Paper scraps dropped around us as we sat on the floor of her bedroom releasing stylish ladies, poised and ready, from the pages. We chose them carefully; their sizes and stances had to fit the outfits we would choose, attached to them by snipped tabs at their shoulders and waists. We shopped and cut out entire wardrobes for our paper ladies. Then we handpicked for them husbands; smartly dressed, handsome men who also gained extra slacks, shirts, and suits. If there was time, we paged through the children's section to lift out younger ones and older ones to join our well-dressed families. But the ladies and their wardrobes were the most engaging.

Indian Cove was mostly Mennonite families. We were folks who stood out for our plain dress that side-stepped fads and fashions to show that we were *in the world but not of it.* "Beauty is only skin deep," we were told. Our beauty was to shine out from the inside of us, so we would add no jewelry or makeup, and wear our skirt hems lower than the dictates of the day. Our hair was left uncut and done up in braids, French or plain.

The matter of hair style came to bother me greatly, and my school notebook sketches and doodles played with the female profile, showing bangs and bouffants added to soften and enhance whatever nose or lips a girl might unluckily have to wear. My sisters and I induced waves into the front of our own hair with water and bobby pins, followed by sticky hair spray. We teased up lift on top the best we could. But, alas, red hair was *not* 'in' at the time, and was so rare that my 7th grade classmates were astounded to learn that I was *not* related to the only other redhead at King Hill School.

As I glanced at my face in the mirror, I noticed that my nose seemed to be growing increasingly

"Maxie," first grade

Vesta, first grade

"Max," third grade

Vesta, third grade

bulbous and that my smile was over-sized and out-of-bounds with a lower lip that made room for overboard front teeth. One boy even called me 'Buckie.' In contrast, Cousin Vesta was blessed with brown hair that tendrilled around her face and created a lower hair line to nicely frame her delicate features. I tried in vain to hold my mouth into the small coy lip shape she wore. *Why must my smile take over my whole face?!* One day on the school bus, Mark from down the road asked me, "Does your face hurt?" My literal-minded answer was quickly punched with his, "Well, it's sure killing me!" I should have known better, because he was the biggest tease, but I quickly forgave him when he exclaimed, "There is gold in your hair!" But, no amount of practice or pinching or wishing could reshape my "Maxie" features.

Sears Roebuck continued to bring Vesta and me paper dolls and a window into fashion. One day, I heard that the Kauffman family had to move to Oregon! I could not imagine how we would do without them; how the Cove could ever go on being what it was, without Kauffman cousins. The farm auction day came, and every farm thing was laid out, numbered, and sold. Their long green chest freezer and the upright piano moved to our house. And then they were gone.

Eventually, we would all move further down the road of time. I came to see it the way our mamas said it: that real beauty comes from within. Over the years, when we visited our relations in the Willamette Valley, I saw that the Kauffman sisters were growing in both kinds of beauty. And Vesta passed on her fashion wisdom to me, showing me an admirable wardrobe hung in her upstairs bedroom closet. She explained that 'more' wasn't necessarily 'better,' because a few carefully chosen and custom-sewn outfits, well cared for, are far better than a whole closet full of clothes. She had selected hers just as diligently as we had for our Sears Roebuck ladies! But Cousin Vesta's beauty would deepen far beyond their poise and fashion.

Later, when we had grown up, and she came back to the Cove for a visit with her baby girl, I would marvel at the calm and graceful motherhood I would see before me. She would explain to me that she focused on contentment, because this was what she wanted most to give her daughter. She would eventually have three more babies, all with picture-perfect mouths, and all blessed with their mother wrapping them in as much contentment as she could.

Vesta became a partner in a mail-order business, where she used her creative gifts to make the catalogs, with the illustrations and her artwork, and then laid it out for printing; a grown-up graphic designer at work.

When we lost her in a tragic drowning, I returned from her memorial service, wanting only to find a catalog somewhere, to cut out paper ladies and search for just the right outfits for them. My custom-made cousin had moved on, again, and I was left to continue crafting my own road to beauty and contentment.

Custom-Made Cousins

Vesta's sister, Betty (Maggie), would have known the song that asks, "Can she bake a cherry pie, Billy Boy?" She made rolling out a pie crust easy with this recipe.

Pie Crust

3 cups flour
1 tsp. salt
1¼ cups shortening
1 egg, beaten
1 tsp. vinegar
5–6 T. water

Mix flour and salt together, and cut in shortening until mixture has pea-sized lumps. Whip up an egg with a fork, mix in the vinegar and water, and add the wet ingredients into the dry. Then use your hands to lightly press into a ball. Do not over-mix!

To roll out, use half the dough for each crust. Press it into a mound on a lightly-floured table, and dust the rolling pin, as well. Press down and roll outward, until the dough is larger than the pie pan. Fold in half to place into the pan. Trim around the edge with a knife and crimp with a twist of your thumb and forefinger.

For a pre-baked pie shell, bake at 425 °F for 10 minutes in a steel or aluminum pan, or 400 °F for glass or ceramic, followed by 375 °F until lightly brown. (For a filled pie, find a recipe that suits your fancy.)

Cinnamon Sugar Pie: Use scraps of dough for a quick treat. Roll out or press the dough into the bottom of pie dish, with no regard for its shape. Sprinkle with sugar, cinnamon, and a little water or milk to moisten. Bake as for a pre-baked pie shell. Enjoy while warm!

Oh, Where Have You Been,
Billy Boy, Billy Boy?

Oh, where have you been,
Billy Boy, Billy Boy?
Oh, where have you been, Charming Billy?
I have been to seek a wife,
She's the joy of my life,
She's a young thing,
And cannot leave her mother.

Did she ask you to come in,
Billy Boy, Billy Boy?
Did she ask you to come in, Charming Billy?
Yes, she asked me to come in,
There's a dimple in her chin.
She's a young thing,
And cannot leave her mother.

Can she make a cherry pie,
Billy Boy, Billy Boy?
Can she make a cherry pie, Charming Billy?
She can make a cherry pie,
Quick as a cat can wink an eye,
She's a young thing,
And cannot leave her mother.

How old is she,
Billy Boy, Billy Boy?
How old is she, Charming Billy?
Three times six and four times seven,
Twenty-eight and eleven,
She's a young thing,
And cannot leave her mother.

Chapter 6

Scaredy Cats
& Their Prayers

THE FEARS OF CHILDHOOD take their various shapes from the contours of our surroundings and the times in which we live. In the Cove, we knelt down at bedtime and prayed:

Now I lay me down to sleep,
I pray the Lord my soul to keep,
If I should die before I wake,
I pray Thee Lord my soul to take.

Perhaps this prayer came from earlier generations when children were more apt to die, because *our* sense of danger was only lightly sprinkled over our everyday lives. Death seemed quite remote. We had heard about Emil Johnson being struck by a lightning bolt while riding in his wagon, but that was way before our time. A grown-up getting cancer or a heart attack occasionally rocked the community. But the Cove had no cemetery, and

Grandpa Hooley's grave marker up in Mountain Home wasn't something I was aware of until I was older.

Scary times were when we heard talk about bombs and bomb shelters during the Cuban Missile Crisis. My sister and I shared a wooden box bed on the floor, and our house had no hallways, so we could hear the grown-ups discussing things right through the wall and closed door. She whispered, "You're too little to understand," when I asked her about it. I didn't take time to argue with her, because I wanted to hear more of what was being said out there.

Even with talk of war, we had a strong sense of God's care, and our cellar was stocked with jars of food. I think Daddy took down some jugs of water, so I figured we were pretty much ready, just in case. We were used to fighter jets from the Mountain Home Air Force Base streaking overhead, thundering out to the practice bombing range south of us, but they did seem more ominous during those days.

Hansel and Gretel and Little Red Riding Hood's plights were known and deliciously scary to us, but as we all know, everything ends up just fine for each and all of them. Our home had no television window to bring us images that could sneak fear in with them, and we knew no spooks at Halloween time. For us, it was the boogey man, the animal kingdom, and the nightly darkness that shaped our childhood fears.

Our boogey man had the uncanny power to grab innocent imaginations and send us flying through the dark, or racing up the open cellar steps, barely touching down. It made feet jump into bed, lickety-split. My oldest brother had hunches about the one in the closet or under the bed in the boys' room, with its appetite for dangling legs and arms. He could be depended upon to notify our younger brothers of a boogey man presence, warning with his "better-not-disturb-it" kind of voice. However, the suspected boogey man showed up mostly in our teasing.

"Oh, what are you afraid of, the boogey man?!"

"You scaredy cat!"

Our farmyard provided scary moments for us, too. I once needed a rescue from a rooster relentlessly chasing me round and round inside the chicken house. Then there was the big dog that accompanied a neighbor who'd had Daddy weld some farm equipment for him. While the men worked, little brother Gary teased the dog from the safety of the cattle loading chute, with "Here, Siegert, Siegert, Siegert!" too young to know that "Siegert" was the farmer's name, and not the dog's.

Add *bulls* to the top of that list of scary animals. When Daddy wintered a herd of Charolais cattle with a mighty, dirt-pawing bull, I had to survive that charging beast in my dreams. Each time, I was hampered with slow-motion running and a yell without a holler. Yet it was only some crazy dream-rabbit that sent me crawling into bed with Mama for safety, one last time.

Bounded by fields and fences, we could count on playing without fear, all the day long. But, then came the night. The darkness could be great fun if there were other children outside, too, like when we chased around parked cars after the Sunday night service, or played "No Bears Out Tonight" in the front yard. But alone in a darkness that was thick and close enough to grab your heels, 'scaredy cat' time came alive!

Closing the chicken house door was a nonchalant walk, at dusk, unless it had suddenly become way too dark. Then, returning to the house while being pursued by some lurking presence required full speed, and a quick duck under the hot wire fence to get to that closed screen door, which opened only on the rebound. More than once, Dale snuck out when he saw me head for the chicken house in the dark, waiting for me in the tree overhead in order to deliver the bobcat cry as I passed under it.

Night's scariest task,
To close the chicken house door
Under knavery!

The howls of the coyotes heard from the safety of our beds were a spine-tingling thrill. The cry of the bobcat would have been the scariest of all the night sounds. Not that we had ever seen one around, but we'd heard tell that bobcats climb trees; make the sound of a crying baby, and then wait to pounce on unsuspecting folks who'd go out to try to rescue the pitiful baby. This wasn't just wild animal fierceness we were dealing with, but the sense of a looming evil. I heard Fan Schrock tell about the grandma who encountered a bobcat at Succor Creek over beyond Jordan Valley and just shook her apron at it, to shoo it away. I figured the grandma may have carried authority because of her age, but I knew that it would be a very different story for any of us small people.

Now, Mama was always nearby, there at the sink, in the garden, sewing, hanging out the clothes, or doing whatever Mamas did back then, and we played securely contented. However, one evening, Mama had to leave us to go check on the irrigation water in the back-forty for Daddy. We would have played and been just fine, except for the cry of the bobcat.

"Did you hear that?"

"H-h-hear what?"

"That bobcat!"

"Oh, I can h-h-hear it, too!"

We were very sure we had heard it. So sure, in fact, that we took refuge in the safest room of the house: the bathroom. It had the washing machine next to the shower that stood between us and the window, and so we crawled up on its top, as many as could fit, after locking the door. We were safe and would wait it out for Mama to return.

"But... what about Mama out there with the bobcat?!" We would have to go out to her, to warn her, to be with her. So we armed ourselves with what weapons we could find—the toilet plunger, the mop, broom, a shovel—and left the safety of the house, holding tightly together in a line, to make our way down the middle of the road to meet Mama in the gathering dusk. She was pretty amazed at the little army coming to meet her, and she told us that, "No..." she had not heard or seen any bobcat. I think she was touched that we had braved danger to protect our mama.

It was one of those good blessings that we Cove children had no greater fears than these country varieties. We thrived in the safety we knew, surrounded by the arms of our parents, our valley, and our Heavenly Father.

Through missionary stories we heard of the dark jungles of Africa. I figured that our soothing lullaby would work for all children, no matter where they might live in the world, whatever their fears might be, since Jesus loves all the children of the world:

> *God takes care of me everyday,*
> *When I run about and play,*
> *And at nighttime when I sleep,*
> *God takes care of me.*

Comfort Foods

Comfort foods are those that 'hit the spot' and make us feel very warm, safe, and loved. They are foods that were served to us by caring hands when we were ill or upset, or simply those times when we all sat around a supper table together. Suppers were often made up of these warming foods, at our house.

A homemade soup or pudding can be stirred up in short order, and, although not as easy as store-bought, the textures and flavors are worth the extra time, which may very well be the reason they are so full of comfort. These foods are rooted in our caring family experience.

Puddings

Mama described for us how Auntie Norma made big bowls full of pudding for her family. 'Pug-gin' is what they called it. Mama came from the Willamette Valley of Oregon to help her sister Norma here in the Cove with her growing houseful of new, little, and bigger children. Spending time in the Cove is how Mama came to know that handsome, Mennonite bachelor farmer. After marrying Daddy she settled down in the valley, where she also made big bowlsful of warm pudding for her own little, and then bigger, children.

2 T. flour or cornstarch
½ cup sugar
A pinch of salt

2 cups scalded hot milk
2 beaten egg yolks (Save the egg whites for home-made Angel Food Cake.)
1 tsp. vanilla
1 T. butter

In a sauce pan, mix flour or cornstarch with sugar and a pinch of salt. Stir in scalded hot milk and beaten egg yolks. Cook over low heat, stirring constantly until thickened. Remove from heat and add 1 teaspoon vanilla and 1 tablespoon butter. Serve warm or cold, and as a "leftover," if there should be any left over.

For Chocolate Pudding: Add 2 T. cocoa with the sugar. Serve warm with milk poured on top.

For Butterscotch Pudding: Use brown sugar instead of white, and sprinkle a little brown sugar on top.

Fruit Cobbler

1 cup flour
1 cup sugar
1 tsp. baking powder
½ tsp. salt
½ cup milk
2 T. butter, softened
2–3 cups canned or fresh fruit

Preheat oven to 350 °F.

Sift dry ingredients together and then add milk and butter, mixing until smooth. Pour fruit into a greased casserole and pour the batter on top.

Bake for about 45 minutes. Serve warm with milk!

Chapter 7

Country School Days

HAMMETT WAS A LITTLE BERG on the main state highway that stretched between the neighboring states of Oregon, Montana, and Wyoming. A turn south from Hammett takes folks to the Snake River and Indian Cove. Farming communities and towns are spread out all along the state highway, with plenty of desert space between them. All share the great ancient lava flow that produced our fine farming soil. The last piece of I-80 to be built, which would complete the stretch across the entire width of the USA, was the section northeast of Hammett, where the valley narrows to the winding Snake River. There, extra measures had to be taken to shore up canyon hills for safe passage, so, for a little while longer, Hammett remained a friendly option for stopping. When the interstate began to swoop drivers across southern Idaho, bypassing all its little towns, Hammett became—for most folks—just a dot on the Idaho map.

For us growing up in Indian Cove, nearby Hammett kept on serving us just fine. Like any small town in those days, it had a little post office, a grocery store, a service station with real mechanics, a school, a grassy park, the Coffee Cup Café and Motel, and an ice cream stand that opened in summertime. There was also the Koch Lumber Company with building materials and farming equipment. For some unknown reason, Hammett didn't have a church until later on, so folks drove to Glenns Ferry or came nine miles our direction, to the church in the Cove. If your family was Seventh Day Adventist, like our neighbors and friends were, well, that meant driving clear up to Mountain Home.

Back in Daddy's day, children went to school on horseback or their own two feet (their "shanks' horses," Mama called them). Walking made sense when their little country school was right there in the Cove, but then it moved out to Hammett. Some days, Daddy drove the Model T and gave rides to his friends Siegert Johnson and Joy Barber. For us, school was a bus ride away, the "Yellow Worm" faithfully carrying Cove children out to Hammett, to King Hill, to Glenns Ferry, and back home again.

I didn't know that two-story brick school houses with silo fire escapes were built all across the country in the fifties. I only knew and loved our own Hammett School. My memories of days there line up like contented children; all the essentials for play were waiting for us at recess, and all the good basics were administered inside by kind and respectable teachers.

The school and the park across the street were tended to by Mr. Wheeler Ladd and his son, Bud. Whether in his irrigation boots, shouldering a shovel, or pushing a wide dust mop across the school's wood floors, Mr. Ladd walked the same unhurried stride, his pants having very little behind him for riding on, and plenty to duck under in front. A hand-rolled cigarette hung from his lips, and the smell of smoke lingered about him. Gruff as he seemed, we knew Mr. Ladd cared about us, for he would come early to start the furnace and get the radiators popping to heat up the classrooms all the way to their high ceilings. He even set the heavy pot of white beans that soaked overnight onto the stove first thing in the morning for Mrs. Reeves, our cook. Mr. Ladd stood leaning forward on his shovel to watch us play at recess. He saw us roller skate, play hop scotch, baseball, marble games, hula hoop, jump rope, and do all the swinging, sliding, and merry-go-rounding in the back school yard. I was surprised as could be when Mr. Ladd gave me a quick 'welcome back' hug against his great paunch after our family returned from wintering in Arizona one year. "Wow, he really missed me!" I thought. Feeling 'special' to Mr. Ladd mixed in with all the other good feelings I had at Hammett School.

One day, someone came up with the ingenious idea of weaving houses in the stand of willow saplings in the empty lot just off the playground. This opened a wondrous kind of play for us at school. Sadly, our project was to be short lived, for we were reined in and confined to the school yard. For me, the injustice of it all grew a child-size discomfort that things do not always make sense in this world of ours. Oh, how I wanted to speak up! But who would listen, who cared, and who could change this rule at school that squelched our ingenuity and industry? We tried our best to somehow build little houses along the tree row inside the play ground, but real estate values plummeted, and we went back to the cycle of roller skates, marbles, hula hoops, jump ropes, and baseball games. Ernie's record-setting swings took baseballs clear over the fence and off the school grounds. Sometimes we had wild episodes of Cowboys and Indians, with Edna Hotchkis as our long-legged horseman, who lead swift flights from pursuing Indians.

Mrs. Ludden's 1st & 2nd grade class (1956)

This Hammett school of ours was especially endowed with gifted students who brought good times for us all. We joined efforts in first grade to use our new phonetic skills and, together, cracked the word "mayonnaise." It dawned on me that 'sounding things out' was an amazing tool, given us at our school. Wilma Shatoe's chalk flying across the blackboard left barely discernible—but totally correct—numerals for our times-tables relay races. And those sixth grade boys intrigued me so when they suddenly became so big and so very handsome!

One year, my class became the older students, and we moved up the long stairs to the second floor. We quickly got over our 'cootie' fears to sing a teasing song to each other in music class, with Mrs. Feeney grinning and pounding it out on the piano.

(BOYS sing first verse.)
Rachel, Rachel, I've been thinking,
What a great world this would be,
If the girls were all transported,
Far across the Northern Sea.

(GIRLS sing this one.)
Reuben, Reuben, I've been thinking,
What a great world this would be,
If the boys were all transported,
far beyond the Northern Sea.

Moving up to fifth and sixth grade made us as mature as we could be. That didn't mean we couldn't cry quietly in our seats when Mrs. Thompson read *Where the Red Fern Grows*, but it did result in being close enough to the principal's office to witness occasional paddlings, which did seem to be justly executed, and which perhaps helped some of us grow up a bit more.

Our upstairs classroom was half of the entire school building. From the ceiling there hung a big, stunning curtain mural that could be lowered to make staging for our Christmas programs. There was plenty of room for learning folk dancing, too, though I sat those out, since we Mennonites didn't dance. Oh, but I did secretly glow when Miles asked me to dance, and in such a gentlemanly way! One day, Mrs. Thompson hauled up a large box and a bunch of dirt for us to sculpt a Peruvian landscape. There, we dispatched our swift imaginary runners on deep canyon trails and over swinging foot bridges, carrying messages from the heights of the Inca Empire to its lower reaches. Clearly the message for us was that learning was more interesting when we could work out of our seats.

One summer, we heard talk that the school children in the Cove would be bussed west, instead of east, to attend school in Bruneau. I was horrified at this thought, knowing that Bruneau folks had cowboys and a tavern in their town. I guess I thought this made the children different in some strange way I couldn't relate to. I didn't know who to thank when the decision was made to keep us in school at Hammett, but I surely was relieved. Hammett school would come to stand empty, one day, but not before I did my junior high years at that distant, dismal King Hill School where we all became 'consolidated.' I don't think I was the only child whose heart protested from the moment we left Hammett School, "But small is better!" Alas, we knew no one who would listen who both cared and could do something about it.

If we could have paid tribute before we all left our little country school, surely we would have done so for Mr. Ladd, for our teachers: Mrs. Ludden, Mrs.

McMillan, Mrs. Lumm, Mrs. Thompson, and our Principal, Mr. Watson. We would have shown our big appreciation for sweetly smiling Mrs. Reeves and her fine home-cooked lunches in the cool basement cafeteria, and our respect for Mr. Petersen who always stayed so calm as he drove our bus. We would have said "Adiós" to Señor Jenkins, and sang once more for Mrs. Feeney, "Oh beautiful for spacious skies...!"

Hammett held our school days; our dear old *golden rule days*.[1] It gave to us the readin', the writin', and the 'rithmetic, along with all of the goodness that only a country school can give.

---

[1] "School Days," *When We Were a Couple of Kids*, by Will Cobb & Gus Edwards (1907).

Chapter 8

Enough for Jake

MR. KIM CAME TO AMERICA from Korea as a visiting teacher at our King Hill Junior High School. He moved around the classroom, up and down between the desks, wafting Old Spice wherever he went. The smell I knew on Daddy was the punchy smells of machine grease and gasoline. I had never known the likes of Mr. Tae Rim Kim's fragrance, and I was all eyes and ears and nose in class, giving him my full swoony attention.

Figuring Mr. Kim might want to see more of our America and how I lived with my farm family in Indian Cove, I asked Mama if I could invite him to come to our house for Sunday dinner. "Why, sure," she said.

Mr. Kim seemed grateful for the invitation. After dinner, we children took him on a little excursion to the Bruneau Sand Dunes. These sand dunes topped all, I figured, and so we directed him there in his little car. The sand dunes are seen to the south once the car leaves the west end of the valley and starts down the grade into Eagle Cove. To the right is the mute rock-rimmed butte withholding its secrets, and to the left beyond the irrigated fields sit the dunes, the tallest and smaller sizes.

We climbed a dune with Mr. Kim, and then we demonstrated for him the two ways to get back down: long, leaping strides could take us to the bottom in a matter of seconds, or rolling down would take a bit longer, but leave us so dizzy we couldn't sit up. We showed both to Mr. Kim, and he took the leaping way, though a bit less leapy than we did it. "Isn't this grand, Mr. Kim!" He flashed us his big, handsome, smiling eyes.

When Mr. Kim was ready to leave the dunes, we soon realized that we had let him pull off the gravel roadway when he had parked his car. His tires spun down into the sand and the car quickly became completely stuck! We calmed his distress by piling out to help push the car until the tires grabbed some gravel. "No problem, Mr. Kim!" I thought triumphantly. I decided this just might have made his day, this adventure in the desert of southern Idaho, USA.

We didn't think to tell Mr. Kim, that afternoon, about how our pioneering Daddy had conquered the sands of the desert for our Indian Cove farm. Daddy could have described how the dunes had been tall enough to completely hide the Caterpillar tractor from view while grading the land. He could have explained how he had to work hard to mix the sand with the clay soil beneath, so it could hold water. It took a lot of crafting the land just right so gravity could move the Snake River water from the canal and the ditches into our fields, and down each corrigate to the hay, the grain, the pinto beans, the sugar beets.

I didn't figure Mr. Kim was up for a hike to the top of the rim that day, to look out over the valley. He would have seen the river flowing into the valley at one end and back out through the canyon on the other end, and his eyes could have followed the canal carrying the river's water to each of its farms. Back when Daddy was a boy, his family had moved here from the edge of the Dust Bowl in Colorado, anticipating new farmland and irrigation. Then, when his Daddy, Paul, suddenly died of a stroke, his mother, Alta, and her strong, hardworking boys went ahead with the project. But I was not yet aware of all this, so sharing the Bruneau Sand Dunes with Mr. Kim was the 'big deal' that Sunday.

Should Mr. Kim have looked around and asked us where the Indians were in Indian Cove, well, we would have stared at him quite blankly, for we had been told nothing about the people who had lived or hunted there, long before our time. But he didn't let on that he had expected to see any.

Some time before my fascination with Mr. Kim, Jake Reimer from Ukraine was our unusual and interesting neighbor. As American children, we knew about the Statue of Liberty holding the light of invitation out to people from other countries who came to find something they needed—like land, work, or freedom. Jake Reimer had been rescued by the Mennonite church in America, when young men in Russia were being forced to fight for the new Czar. The Mennonite farming communities there were rapidly losing their freedom to stay unarmed farmers, and were being harmed for not cooperating with the new demand. Jake's friendly accent, his rich coloring, his manners, even the train conductor-like hat he wore, fascinated us children.

When Mama took me down to visit Jake's wife Leona, he was out somewhere working hard on his well-kept place there beside the river. Leona served us cookies, with her gentle warm smile, and sang a little song for me.

> I'm a lonely little Petunia in the onion patch,
> The onion patch, the onion patch.
> I'm a lonely little Petunia in the onion patch,
> Oh, why won't you come and play with me?
> Boo hoo; boo hoo!
> I'm a lonely little Petunia in the onion patch,
> Oh, why won't you come and play with me!

I liked singing Leona's sweet, sad song, especially the "boo hoo" part. I wondered if she might be lonely, not having any children of her own to play with. Or perhaps Jake was the one who felt like the Petunia, surrounded by acres of fairer-skinned farmers; a lonely Russian Mennonite among Swiss German and English folks. He didn't come to church. Daddy thought it might be because of his smoking—something maybe okay for Mennonites in Ukraine, but not so here.

After a meal at the family table, anything left over was considered to be "just enough for Jake." I asked Mama once if that meant Jake could have joined us for dinner; that there would have been plenty for him, too. She said it didn't mean our Cove's Jake, or anyone in particular; only that we had enjoyed a plentiful meal that could have been shared with a guest. I thought that was a good idea we might do more often, like we did for Mr. Kim.

Dinner from Garden and Cellar

Farm dinners were usually 'meat and potato' meals, in typical Idaho tradition. Mashed potatoes can be served up with a gravy made from the meat drippings, but this needn't always be so. Cucumber Goomer Slaw, a tomato gravy, or homemade sauerkraut are gifts from the garden to put over potatoes, making a hearty farm dinner.

Cucumber Goomer Slaw

I called it "Goomer Salaw." This cucumber dish frequented our summer table, alongside freshly boiled potatoes.

2 large fresh cucumbers, peeled and sliced thin
½ onion, sliced thin
1 tsp. salt, at least
½ cup cream, sour cream, or mayonnaise

Sprinkle the cucumbers liberally with salt, and place a plate over them for 30 minutes. Then squeeze out the cucumbers and rinse off the salt.

Fold cucumber and onion slices into the dressing.

Serve as is, or refrigerate for 8–12 hours.

Tomato Gravy

Tomato gravy is wonderful when spooned over mashed potatoes!

2 cups tomato juice
2 T. flour
Salt to taste
A little soda—about ½ tsp.
Sugar to taste
Milk to desired thickness

Heat tomato juice. Stir in soda. Mix flour with a little milk and stir into warmed tomato juice. Add a little sugar to taste—maybe 1 or 2 teaspoons for a pint of juice, and add milk as desired.

Before serving, add white crackers, slightly broken. But don't add them too early before serving, or else the crackers will get soggy!

Tomato Catsup

Making catsup is one of those tasks in autumn that blesses the family meals all year long—or until it runs out!

4 quarts tomato juice
3 cups vinegar
3½ cups sugar
¼ cup canning salt
1 cup onion, diced
½ tsp. of each:
    cloves, cinnamon, ginger, nutmeg, red pepper

Mix ingredients and simmer until thick. Stir occasionally. You may want to use a slow cooker, or roast in oven.

Ladle catsup into jars. They do not need to be sealed, but it helps keep the top of the catsup from turning dark. Mama sealed it, unless the newly filled jar went directly into the refrigerator for immediate use.

Chapter 9

New Clover in our Patchwork Cove

"HAVE YOU SEEN THEM YET?" we asked Daddy. Of course he would be the first to meet the new family, since he was out and about in the valley, exchanging crop and water talk with the neighboring farmers of the Cove.

"And, did you see their girl?"

The Blacks came from the land of Bruneau, that valley southwest of our Cove. To drive to Bruneau, one must go up and out the west end of our valley and past Rio Vista and the Sand Dunes, and then leave the Snake River to go up over and down to where the Bruneau River flows. It was a world away from our Cove Valley! We would sometimes skirt past Bruneau's small-blink-of-a-town and along its farmland edge when making our way to the Indian Bathtub or Bruneau Canyon. Farmers there were called ranchers, and there were cowboys, too.

Growing up in the Cove, we had never seen cowboys or a rodeo, and now our valley had a cowboy-rancher family moving into the middle of it. The Blacks had bought the Kauffman farm, settled into our cousins' house, and, before we knew it, range cattle and horses replaced the dairy cows, chickens, and pigs in the pens and barns Uncle Vernon had so proudly built.

And there was another thing: The Blacks were Catholic. We had never known any Catholics in the Cove. We were a valley of mostly Sunday-go-to-meetin' Mennonites and Sabbath-observin' Seventh Day Adventists. These Blacks would be an entirely new flavor for us.

In this new family, there were lots of boys, but only one girl. "Imagine that!" We sisters considered this fact amazing. The Kauffmans were a big family, too, but they had half and half, boys and girls. So, at the end of another summer vacation, we watched in anticipation as the school bus hesitated at the end of their lane. One by one, the Black boys got on, from younger to older. And then, there she was: tall, with long dark hair and smiling eyes; looking like a rodeo queen with a rancher-family stride! I imagined she must have held an especially strong bond with her mother against such an onslaught of brothers, or maybe a high code of chivalry existed in her family of high-ridin' cowboys—one that granted her a pedestal place. I tried to picture her life and wished I were a little watching mouse in that cinder block house.

Celia's bright friendly smile soon became regular fare for us every morning on the bus ride to school. One day I noticed that my brother had scooped up more than his fair share of those smiles.

In secret fascination I watched as her laughing dark eyes caught his. *She knows how to flirt!* I was amazed. Although it may have gone on around me, I'd paid it no mind, and I certainly did not know how to do it! Yet, here it was before me, as real as a butterfly's flitting dance.

Since our fields touched at the fenceline along the east side of our farm, I considered it my sisterly duty to keep my brother's secret when I knew why he stopped the tractor over by the fence. That much I could do.

From the top of the rimrock on the west side of the valley, the fields below vary in hue, size, and shape. They spread out from the river's willow-lined edge, to the south where shades of greens and yellows give way to the sage of the sandy desert range. In spring, our valley is surrounded on three sides by the green of new cheatgrass[1] that blushes vermilion and pink, and then pales to a soft gold. It is all a quilt, where colors and textures meet and change at fence rows. And, just as the patchwork of the connecting fields is traced through by the arteries of a canal and the irrigation ditches, we children liked to draw out a 'family tree' that also had branches reaching out to connect the folks in the Cove with our Hooley family, making them all our relations. We had extended this activity to almost everyone in the valley, so now we would do

---

[1]Cheatgrass grows in the sandy deserts of North America's Great Basin. It probably arrived here in contaminated grain from Europe in the late 1890's. Cheatgrass seed heads look like a shepherd's crook, and they irritate everyone by catching onto any sock or hairy dog's ear that passes through it.

it to include the new family, too.

Let's see. Great Uncle Noah came west after his wife Jenny had died, and he married the Cove's "Old Maid" Fan Shenk. Fan is the sister to Dave, Amos, and Tim. A nephew of Amos' wife Viola married one of the Blacks over in Jordan Valley, which meant *we were related!* Totally satisfied, we concluded there was definitely a place in the Cove family for our new neighbors, the Blacks.

Celia's mom, Margaret, opened up her home to make a special new thing in our young lives. It was called "4-H." We had a real—not a pretend—club, with meetings and officers, and even a four-leaf-clover club pledge. My 4-H projects expanded to forestry and entomology, as I searched beyond the valley's common Locusts and Elms for my tree leaf collection, and pushed pins through stink bugs and butterflies, all chloroformed and mounted into a cigar box.

In Margaret's living room, we sewed aprons and crafted button-holes and zippers by hand. Simple fashions were made to wear. We wrote everything up in our record books with the green four-leaf clover on the covers. We held our breath near the end of the summer as we raced to finish everything in time for the Elmore County Fair, where there would be all manner of showing and seeing to be done, topped off with that sweet, momentary cotton candy. And there we garnered our blue and red ribbons. Daddy even got into the county fair spirit, showing off his very largest sugar beets and coming home with the prized twenty-five pound sack of sugar from the Amalgamated Sugar Company.

This 4-H club of ours saw to it that the Cove got a road sign; the only sign I think it had ever had, other than my temporary "Rabbits for Sale," posted at the end of our lane. This new sign sat on the west end of the valley where anyone coming from Bruneau could clearly see it, and it read, "Indian Cove 4-Hers Welcome You."

THE 4-H PLEDGE

I pledge my head to clearer thinking,
My heart to greater loyalty,
My hands to larger service,
My health to better living,
for my club, my community,
my country, and my world.

4-H is a County Extension project for children all across the country, in states with land-grant colleges. 4-H was almost six decades old in this country when we had our first 4-H club in the Cove. I just know that Margaret Black is forever a 4-Her at heart, because she has done what the good pledge says to do, in creating her many quilts. She has seen to it that the Idaho Historical Society *captures quilts in time, offering each one a number and a place in the annals of Idaho history, recorded as a valuable work of art for now and for later.*

Recipes from the Neighbors

Whether bringing in a dish to show they cared, or helping with a building project, good neighbors were one of those huge blessings the Cove held for us.

More Casserole

Jan Hampton made us "More" after Mama's mastectomy, and she sent her teenage son Frank to bring it over for us. We could clearly understand why it was called "More!" We promptly got the recipe from her so we could make More when we needed a hearty casserole. Cooking with a can of pimentos was new to us, and it adds to the colors that make this dish attractive to serve to guests.

Prepare 8 ounces spaghetti

Fry together:
1 lb. hamburger
½ lb. sausage
1 onion
1 green pepper
1 stalk celery
Chopped garlic
1 can tomatoes with puree
Couple tsp. flour for thickening

Spread spaghetti in shallow, garlic-rubbed pans. Spread over it a drained can of each of these:
Peas, ripe olives, pimentos, and mushrooms.

Pour over spaghetti the meat mixture and tomato puree, mixing slightly with fork.

Sprinkle with cheese and heat thoroughly in oven.

.

Meatballs or Meat Loaf

Whatever you use to fix your meatballs or meat loaf, be sure to serve with applesauce. When Tim Shenk came to help Daddy build an addition onto our house to expand it for our expanding family, Mama served meatballs. Tim asked where the applesauce was, and Mama promptly produced applesauce from the canning shelves in the cellar. We served these two together, ever after.

1 lb. ground beef
Onion, chopped
Handful saltine crackers, crushed
¼ cup milk, or so
1 egg
Salt and pepper

Mix together and form into balls for meatballs, or into a loaf pan for meat loaf. Prepare topping, below.

¼ cup catsup, or so
Couple T. mustard
Couple T. brown sugar

Squirt catsup and mustard right onto the unbaked meatloaf, and add brown sugar. Mix it around on the meatloaf with a spoon, and bake at 350 °F for half-hour, or until done.

For meatballs, add a little water and a couple teaspoons vinegar to the topping mixture. Pour over meatballs in the pan after they have been browned. Put on lid to finish cooking.

Chapter 10

Our Auntie

IF YOU LIVED miles and miles away from any of your aunts, uncles, and grandparents, like we did in Idaho, then you would do well to have an auntie who could come and go, to visit and stay awhile. My Mama's sister, Eunice King, was ours.

"Aunt Eunie" lived in the Willamette Valley in Oregon. She grew up the youngest in the King family, with her three brothers and three sisters: Uncle Lyle, Uncle Howard, Uncle Hadley (who drowned when he was ten), Auntie Norma, Auntie Bill (Beulah), and our mama, "Dot." Only for Aunt Eunie did we drop the 'ie' off *auntie* so we could add it to her name, making her our very own "Aunt Eunie." That is just how unique and special this aunt of ours was to us, growing up in the Cove.

Aunt Eunie traveled in her little blue Rambler, from Oregon's naturally green Willamette Valley to our Cove Valley, made green with irrigation. For years she drove that car back and forth to see us. Grandpa and Grandma King[1] often came with her

---

[1] Oliver and Florance of Hubbard, Oregon.

on her trips, and so we were brought all of that love in one visit.

When they arrived at our place, Aunt Eunie always jumped right into our lives the moment she got out of her car. Babies were grabbed, rocked, and "chin-chucked," and little ones greeted with some "borey, borey, borey gicks!"[2] Her funny faces quickly compelled any reticent or unhappy child into giggles and smiles. Heads got scrubbed with so much vim and vigor that scalps fairly danced! The pies were in the oven before you knew it, and dinner helped to the table. She just did everything right up.

And her laugh—I remember trying to figure how she did it—her laugh was the hearty kind that comes from down inside and rises to higher and higher notes as it tumbles out. Life just got a little easier and a lot more fun when Aunt Eunie came to stay awhile! And when bedtime descended on our house, she and her pillow—which she always brought with her—would join us sisters in our bedroom, making happy nighttime chatter.

When I was eight, Daddy and Mama loaded us into the 1949 Mercury with a trailer in tow, to take us to the Phoenix, Arizona climate for warmer winter months. Aunt Eunie came down, too, and became our nanny, since Mama was very tired and not well. She just slid right into the family and did whatever was needed to be done, in her loving and predictable way—probably spankings included, though I don't remember any. Daddy told us to mind her like she was Mama, or he would spank us.

---

[2]Don't ask.

And he told Aunt Eunie to make us mind, or she'd be in trouble! I think we all pretty much did just that.

Each afternoon when the ice cream truck came down our street playing its happy melody, Aunt Eunie heard our little pleas and placed a coin in each of our hands. What fun it was to be living in the city with an ice cream truck traveling up and down our street, even in winter!

After we got back to the Cove in spring, a doctor gave Mama special vitamins that helped her feel better. Then, come August, he delivered our healthy and dark-haired baby brother Gene. We had Aunt Eunie to thank for helping us children stay happy and secure during Mama's hard time, while our little brother was being knit together inside her.

Summertimes were rather risky for Aunt Eunie's visits to the Cove because of our bachelor neighbor Dave. He would characteristically drive down the lane very slowly, and if she happened to be outside, he could get a good look at her on his way home from checking his cows out on the range. Aunt Eunie would hunker clear down behind the vegetables when his drive-by caught her in the garden; and when she was unfortunate enough to be in the strawberry patch close by the road, she would have to flatten clear out in a corrugate to hide! We liked it when he stopped by with ice cream and root beer for hot-day floats, or to bring his annual trunk load of sweet melons to share. But as much as we teased Aunt Eunie about him, we did not put either one of them into a predicament.

For a time, Uncle Howard's lived way up in the Athabasca River country of Alberta, and Aunt Eunie drove up one year with Grandpa and Grandma to pay them a visit. Aunt Eunie returned with amazing stories of menacing clouds of mosquitoes and bears lurking nearby the necessary outhouse. I would study the photo of my Canada cousins—the one where they are all standing next to the white fence like sunflowers all in a row—and think about how lucky Aunt Eunie was to be able to travel so far; to such a wild and distant place.

Aunt Eunie entertained us with stories from her nursing days, as well. She told us about those strange long-johns off old geezers in the hospital that could stand up by themselves. We heard of her days in the kitchen at Western Mennonite School, where she fed hungry boarding high school students both hearty food and loving attention. When she went to Mexico to care for babies in an orphanage, her stories gave us a tiny peek into a very different kind of family in a very different place. I felt sad for 'her babies' left behind when she had to return home to care for Grandma.

I came to see this about Aunt Eunie as I grew up: this aunt of ours had a way of spreading blessings over us like a great unfolding fan of contentment and gracious hospitality. As all of the King-begottens begat, more and more, it was as if she had been the welcoming committee for every newcomer, generation after generation. With each wedding, there was a set of her hand-embroidered pillow cases, and then her fingers would fly to make baby quilts. It was as if she had been keeping us all stitched firmly inside the burgeoning and blooming King family tree.

Each family had Aunt Eunie woven somewhere into the warp or woof of their life. We nieces and nephews who lived at a distance, especially needed this. When Daddy drove us to Oregon, I was always shy and nervous about visiting all our Oregon relations over there, but Aunt Eunie's matter-of-factness and congeniality helped to take the edge off of any tense situation. We felt far from home, but when she was around, it was a little easier to be one of the King grandchildren.

Being one of 'the Kings' had given us royalty in our auntie, our one-and-only Aunt Eunie.

To Auntie

Chief of our aunts—not only I,
But all your dozen of nurslings cry—
What did the other children do?
And what were childhood, wanting you?
by Robert Browning

Aunt Eunie's Recipes

Preparing food for those you care about is one of the most substantial ways to love on them. When food was served and the satisfying meal enjoyed, Aunt Eunie's own Mom (our Grandma) would announce to her, "My sufficiency has been sufficiencized!" We could always count on Aunt Eunie for this.

Foods and recipes I associate with Aunt Eunie are satisfying soups and beautiful pies, among the many things she selected from recipe books to fix for us.

Potato Soup

4–5 potatoes, cubed
Bacon (optional)
Couple T. onion, chopped finely
Celery rib, chopped finely
Couple T. butter
2–3 T. flour
1 quart of milk
Salt and pepper, to taste

Sauté onion and celery in butter while preparing the potatoes. Add and cook the potatoes with salt, using enough water to almost cover them in the pan. Do not drain.

Fry a little bacon (or butter), and mix in flour. Stir this into the pot of potatoes. Add milk.

If you want a thicker soup, use cream, or add a little flour mixed with water or milk.

Easy Butter Crust
From *Zion Mennonite Cookbook*

An open 9-Inch pie, perfect for fresh strawberry filling.

1 stick butter or margarine
2 T. sugar
A dash of salt
Scant 1¼ cups flour

Melt stick of butter right in the pie pan. Mix sugar, salt, and flour, and then add this to the butter. Mix well. Pat mixture into the shape of the pie pan. Bake at 350 °F for about 10–15 minutes. Watch closely for desired browning. Fill with favorite pie filling.

Chapter 11

On Chickens & Politics

CLOISTERED in Indian Cove and our small schools, and with no exposure to popular TV culture or the evening news, politics was something only discussed in high school government class. I did have to learn the difference between the words *capitol* and *capital*—one of those spelling tasks, and in fourth grade we were bussed clear to Boise for a tour of Idaho's big marble-domed capitol building. But, the *goings-on* at the state and national capitals were far from our lives.

We children knew our family was Republican, and when voting time came around, Daddy would drive over to the Pancoast's house on the other end of the valley to mark his ballot. I think Mama went with him when we were a little older, but they didn't talk about it together, that I can remember. Other than that, anything political seemed to happen in the barnyard, or on the schoolyard.

In the barnyard the chickens have a pecking order, and at the top of this hierarchy is usually a rooster. We, at one time, had a very handsome and cocky rooster, and, being the respectable Republicans we were, and figuring that he was acting like a Democrat when he pranced around acting so high and mighty, named him *Kennedy*. Kennedy strutted his proud self, and we despised him for it. Mercilessly, our brothers chased him around the house and the barnyard until he was exhausted. One day when he dropped over on the ground and they were scared he had died, they quit pestering him.

I had no idea how it came about, but something changed in the chicken house, after that. Suddenly, our Kennedy became the low-man-on-the-totem-pole. He was quickly reduced to a sorry, scrawny sight as he was picked on by the now-higher-orders of both hens and roosters alike. Then we truly felt sorry for him.

But politics didn't end with *our* Kennedy's downfall. On the playground at school we fought the biggest political campaign battle of the fifties with our loud chants: *Nixon, Nixon, he's our man! He threw Kennedy in the garbage can!* I think the Democrat children in our school were probably out-numbered, and we bantered them with our ditties. But Kennedy became President Kennedy in that election.

One day, at King Hill Junior High, when the clock on the wall showed almost lunch time, a voice interrupted over the intercom, and we heard the principal's voice telling us that President John F. Kennedy had been shot. Frozen in shock, we joined our classmates in the days that followed in mourning with our nation. We had lost the young president who had challenged everyone to ask what they could do for our country, and to quit just thinking about what our country could do for them. I figured he was talking to us in the Cove, too.

While family politics stayed as predictable as the sunrises and sunsets, we were coming to see that some things have a way of changing on us; ruling roosters and national leaders come and go. National politics was catching up with us, even in our little cove world, and I wondered about how changes make us see things a little differently than we had before.

Chapter 12

Bruneau Canyon: A Family Affair

INDIAN COVE SITS between the rimrocks along the south side of the Snake River at the top edge of Owyhee County, a vast county stretching out beyond the fields and farms of our cove. It takes up a big chunk of the map of our Idaho, creating its huge southwest corner. Its expanse is mostly desert, where cows range on BLM[1] land, where the deer and the antelope play, and where jackrabbits compete with the coyotes for the "Most Populous" title each year. A sudden surprising herd of wild horses might be sighted galloping over a ridge in the distance. The United States Air Force flies in formation overhead, using a designated bombing range for target practice. It is a land of mountains and canyons, with the abandoned mines of Silver City, and the Delamar mine still worked today. It is occasioned by ghosts, hunters, and range ranchers on horseback. Those who enter this land are lured

---

[1]Bureau of Land Management.

by silent junipers and quaking aspen, its ghost towns and game, its expeditions and adventures.

One of our family's favorite excursions into Owyhee County is the Bruneau Canyon. Leaving in the early morning with hats, lunches, and water jugs, we head out to the neighboring Bruneau valley and turn south into the desert. After miles of dusty road, and taking into account the distance traveled, we select the set of tire tracks to the right for our encounter with the canyon. It's not visible from the road, but is nestled down a bit over the rise like a sleeping dragon. We must approach it on foot and gaze at it from its sudden drop-off edge. It is a giant cut riven by an act of God when no one was watching. The earth had split open so long ago that it scabbed over into lichen-covered sides that now stand guard over a deeply hidden juvenile river, flowing far below.

After we pay tribute to the view from the edge, we enter the canyon by way of a trail that switchbacks its way to the bottom. Rubbing shoulders with this venerable desert legend demands respectful vigilance. It is a steep trail, but more so, we know that its rock ledges are sunny platforms for coiled rattlesnakes, and its bushes home to hitchiking ticks awaiting a warm-blooded passerby. We descend in single file.

At the bottom of the canyon trail is a green burst of oasis, shadowed between the crowding vertical walls. We shed dusty shoes to dip feet and hands into the cool clear water. There is a unique and compelling stillness here. We speak softly, or not at all. There is time to sit still and to do our reflections at the water's edge, and to eat our lunch. If we could, we might stay forever in this place that is so unaware of any other world above it.

Then we move downstream, or upstream, working around bushes and wading where there is no available bank. Upstream, there is a huge, old juniper tree that must have grown for many years before burning in a desert fire that swept down into the canyon. On the wall behind the tree there is an Indian painting done in red of a man standing by a lady. Was it to signify a sacred spot; a place of commitment; of love's embrace; perhaps a burial? We can't read it, so we don't know.

Only a vague sense of needing to return to our waiting car and our suspended quick-time lives moves us to go back to our shoes, to leave the canyon by retracing our steps up the side of the canyon wall.

The day I took my friend, Betty from Ohio, to view Bruneau Canyon, there wasn't time for a hike down into it, so I would drive her out across the desert just to introduce her to our great, Owyhee County geology. It would be stretched out silently under afternoon sun in the cheatgrass and sagebrush. At its precipitous edge, we exchanged remarks about its geological profundities. Then, I picked up a small rock to show her the canyon's great depth by casting it and watching its long descent. Having skipped upper-level high school science, I was, at that moment, woefully at the mercy of my abysmal lack of a knowledge of physics. With my keys still held in my right hand, and the rock secured between thumb and finger of that same

hand, I flung wide my arm to launch it, whereupon
the unguarded forces-that-be wrenched open my
entire hand. Our eyes left the trajectory of the
rock's flight and locked on my ring of keys that
were now on their own wild path, sailing downward,
and disappearing out of our sight.

If she had been wide-eyed at the impressive
vista, Betty was now standing with eyes gaping.
The canyon was no longer the tame sleeping legend. In one appointed moment it had become the
mythical dragon beast rising from its quiet repose,
to leap and to swallow those keys in one silent and
triumphant gulp!

Betty and I were now stranded, alone. We
walked back to the little two-door green Datsun
and sat. Night would soon spread over us. There
was nothing to do but wait. So, we talked or read
from a pocket-size Gideon New Testament lying on
the console. Looking back, I figure it was prime
time for telling jokes to laugh, but I don't remember
that we did any of that.

Suppertime came and went, and we sat. "*Eventually*, we will be missed," I consoled us both.

Now the car was permeated with the darkness,
and the wind began to push against it. We resisted
the need to open a door to find a proverbial bush,
not wanting to let in the night's gusty chill. The
hours ticked by.

An apology was not needed, I stubbornly decided. *Who could have planned a more memorable
event for a friend's visit to Idaho?* "She may even
decide to thank me for this," I defensively concluded.
Sweet Betty did not have a critical word to say to

me, nor a 'thank you.'

My caring family dispatched two brothers that night to rescue us, and they were amused, but kind. Their kindness became heroic, in my eyes, when the next morning found them returning to the canyon to retrieve the car—and my keys from a ledge below!

Nature in the desert is capricious enough that I think I will never again want to encounter Bruneau Canyon alone, or again as two defenseless (one of us senseless) maidens. For me, Bruneau Canyon will always be *a family affair!*

Satisfying Suppers

Quick suppers come from home-canned goods brought up from the cellar, or frozen foods from the green chest freezer. The warmed leftovers from the supper that Betty and I might have found waiting for us on that Bruneau Canyon night could have been soup, cornbread, or fruit cobbler, as often suppers were at our house. When served with a platter of cheese and pickles, or fresh garden vegetables when in season, this makes a very satisfying evening meal.

Tomato Soup

1 pint canned tomato juice
½ tsp. baking soda
About 1 T. flour mixed with a little cold juice or water
Salt and pepper to taste
Pat of butter

Warm a jar of canned tomato juice in a saucepan, and stir in soda. To thicken, mix flour in cold water or juice, and stir into the soup. Add salt and pepper, and pour in milk to make it as thick or thin as you prefer it. Heat until steaming hot, but don't boil. Top with butter, and serve with saltine crackers.

Pea or Pinto Bean Soup

Grandma King made pea soup for us, and so did Mama, sometimes using pinto beans instead, for a hearty winter soup.

Leftover green peas
Milk
Salt and pepper
Pat of butter

Mash cooked peas or beans in the bottom of a saucepan and add milk to desired consistency. Sprinkle with salt and pepper, and add the pat of butter.

Cornbread
From the Albers Cornmeal box

1½ cups all-purpose flour
⅔ cup sugar
½ cup Albers® White or Yellow Corn Meal
1 T. baking powder
½ tsp. salt
1¼ cups milk
2 large eggs, lightly beaten
⅔ cup vegetable oil
3 T. butter or margarine, melted

Preheat the oven to 350 °F. Grease 8-inch square baking pan. Combine flour, sugar, corn meal, baking powder, and salt in medium bowl. Combine milk, eggs, vegetable oil, and butter in small bowl and mix well. Add to flour mixture, and stir just until blended. Pour into prepared baking pan.

Bake for 35 minutes or until wooden pick inserted in center comes out clean. Serve warm with milk and honey or sugar.

Chapter 13

'Twas That Time in December

'Twas that time in December when all
    through our land,
There was making and baking and get-
    ting things planned.
The folks in the Cove moved into high
    gear,
To pull from traditions, as Christmas
    drew near.

No stockings, no chimney, no nightcaps,
    nor mice,
We folks did it simple; it turned out quite
    nice.
We trekked through the desert to search
    a sage tree,
That's perfect in balance, though just
    three-foot-three.

When shortening-can planted and carried inside,
The sage smelt o'er-powering, but soon
did subside.
The lights scattered through its soft grey-
green hue,
Made decorating together a fun thing to
do.

To send merry wishes and to acknowl-
edge the reason,
We handmade our cards to feature the
season.
*Winds through the olive trees softly did
blow,*
And *Away in a Manger* with those cows
that do low.

Repeating the lines most carefully learned,
With candle-lit faces so sweetly upturned.
Hard candy and oranges in brown paper
sacks
Were passed out to all, for our evening
snacks.

Caroling topped all, sporting long-johns
of gray,
And a tractor—not reindeer—pulled our
wagon away.
Tenor, bass, alto, and soprano on top,
In pitch perfect harmony; each house
was our stop.

We went to the sheep camp and sang
  them in Spanish,
Where Basque sheepherders gave us their
  pass-the-hat wish.
Oft clear into Hammett we drove in our
  cars,
To Hickenlooper's, to Schrock's—to more
  folks than the stars.

The twinkles we captured were not Santa's
  eyes,
—All sprinkled in snow and throughout
  the night skies.
With Brubaker oranges, echoes in our
  heads,
We took cherry noses and turned toward
  our beds.

Christmas Eve was readied, all put into
  play,
With Nativity placed a'top the buffet.
Silhouettes of Wise Men pointing to the
  star,
All taped to the window for each passing
  car.

Each Christmas morn' came, in its own
  special way,
With sharing of gifts and foods made for
  the day.
In-laws were added, and eighteen great
  cousins,

Our family did grow, as did our traditions.

We hand out the bells and our voices unite,
Merry Christmas to all and to all a goodnight!

Mama's Candy

Caramel-colored Peanut Brittle next to snowy white Divinity, alongside homemade Chocolates, together make a Christmas candy platter and sweet holiday tradition.

Peanut Brittle

Have ready:
¼ cup salted butter
½ pound raw peanuts
1 T. soda
1 tsp. vanilla
Large pan or tray, lightly greased

Combine the following ingredients and boil together to the hard-boil stage:
3 cups sugar
1 cup corn syrup
1 cup water

Add the butter and the peanuts. Cook together, stirring constantly, until light brown and the skins pop open on the peanuts. Add the soda and the vanilla, stirring rapidly to mix. Immediately pour onto the greased pan and spread as thinly as possible. Break into pieces and store in a cardboard container to prevent pieces sticking together.

Divinity

4 cups sugar
1 cup corn syrup
1 cup water
½ tsp. salt
2 egg whites
1 tsp. Mapleine, Black Walnut, or Vanilla flavoring
2 cups chopped nuts

Stir sugar, corn syrup, water, and salt together in a saucepan over medium heat, until dissolved. Cover until it starts to boil. Uncover and cook until a firm ball forms when tested in cold water. While cooking, beat egg whites very stiff. Remove candy from heat and slowly add to the egg whites, beating constantly. When mixture begins to thicken (takes awhile) add flavoring and nut meats. Continue beating until it will hold its shape and begins to lose gloss.

Using 2 spoons, drop the divinity onto waxed paper, using 1 spoon to push the candy off the other, twirling the pushing spoon to give the candy the look of a soft-serve ice cream.

If the candy becomes too stiff, add a few drops of hot water. You will need to work fast when making this type of candy.

Penuche Fudge

Mama had this one memorized because she often made Penuche, if not a chocolate fudge, as a Sunday afternoon treat.

1 cup brown sugar
1 cup white sugar
½ cup milk
1 T. butter
1 cup nuts
1 tsp. vanilla
Speck salt

Line a 9-inch square pan with foil; grease foil with 1 tsp. butter.

Mix sugar, milk, butter and salt. Cook until it forms a soft ball when dropped in cold water (234 °F). Cool about 40 minutes, without stirring. Beat with a spoon until fudge begins to thicken. Add nuts and vanilla. Continue beating until fudge becomes very thick and just begins to lose its sheen—about 10 minutes.

Immediately spread fudge into prepared pan. Cool. Lift candy out with the foil and cut into pieces.

Chapter 14

Seeing it Her Way

OUR LITTLE SISTER SHARON came later, and she broke the tie between three brothers and three sisters in our family. She was perfect in every detail, we noted, like a living porcelain doll. We marveled at her delicate features, her tiny fingers and toes, her sweet smile. One day, Auntie Norma told us Sharon wasn't seeing us see her. "How can this be," we puzzled! When Dr. Howard, up in Boise, confirmed this, I realized we had been so caught up that we hadn't noticed she never returned our admiring gazes.

As she grew up, we showed Sharon the world around us:

— Here, Sharon, look at these long seed pods of the locust tree.

— Hold out your hands. See this chick we borrowed from the little banty hen?

— Daddy is smiling.

— The warm sun is yellow; the cool leaves are green.

Sharon came to see things in her own way. With us, she shared what she heard; things we had not heard before. The sounds of music that we were accustomed to were a capella at church, the "Gospel Hour" on the radio, and long-playing "Mennonite Hour" records Grandma Yoder sent to us. Alvin and the Chipmunks once came singing *Christmas, Christmas time is here...*, over and over and over again, from the wind-up record player our cousins loaned us for a day, until Mama forbade us to play it one more time! My sisters and I plunked out keys on the upright piano to match the shaped notes in the hymnal, and we chorded our way through the familiar songs and choruses. The same could be done on the keys of the pearly white and red accordion, which Daddy bought from the door-to-door salesman. Dale strummed pleasing harmonies on his guitar. These had been the sum-total of our musical life, but Sharon was spending hours with the music I'd never heard before—Bach, Beethoven, Debussy, Chopin—on records bought for her. Then a stream of symphonic scores began to flow from her own fingers at the piano, floating through our house. There were also rhythms and percussion from whatever could be lightly tapped. Our quiet farm life had come to have new rhythms and melodies.

One day, Sharon performed compositions of her own making, complete and compelling! Mama and Sharon walked up the road to show Ola what she could do. That was probably the day Mama decided a piano teacher was in order for Sharon.

Our Cove world held a good supply for children to grow up on, and our quiet and unassuming Mama would go out of the valley to find whatever else our little sister needed. Sharon graduated from one piano teacher to the next. Mama drove her up to the Gooding State School for the Deaf and Blind for the school weeks so she could learn to read Braille, and then saw to it that the Glenns Ferry school gave Sharon an assistant to help her with her school work. Surely our parents' prayers to God that He would lead them down a good road for Sharon was how her assistant Fran came to sit beside her desk at school, where she teased a great sense of humor out of her, humor that would help Sharon smooth out some of the bumps in her life.

Relentlessly, Mama wrung the best out of what there was. She saw to it that Sunday School and Vacation Bible School materials Sharon needed were painstakingly brailled, even if she had to do it herself. She read out loud to her, and recorded textbooks onto audio cassettes when necessary. Nothing was permitted to hinder Sharon, so that she could follow the rest of us up and out of the Cove, when the time came.

"Don't tell anyone," Sharon confided. "Everything there is—even you and everybody—has a musical note." We had been walking the road near the Snake River when she told me this. She'd asked me to describe for her the different blues of sky and of river, and I was struggling with words to give the essence—the feeling—of blue colors, and how the river would sometimes reflect the same blue of the sky, and other times look dark and thick; not really blue, at all.

I was taken aback. "You're kidding! What is the river's note, the rimrock, that bird—me, what's my note? How do you do that?" This was something very different from blueness!

"I don't do anything," she explained. "They just *have* them."

"You don't pick the notes? You just know what they are?" I marveled at this startling new dimension suddenly surrounding me. I was certainly coming to see some things in a very different way.

At some point I just had to tell someone else about this revelation, though I don't remember when I let it slip. By this time I had come to like the idea of uniqueness, and so being different from others had become an attractive trait to aspire to. Not so, for her.

"Seriously, Sharon, I would let the world know I had this beautiful mind!"

"You know how it is: The blind have a musical gift, *right?* But I want more than this, don't you see?"

It became plain to me that there's much more to seeing than meets the eye. First, music is a big part of this world of ours, coloring it in multihued ways. Secondly, perspective and understanding must be wider and deeper than I had ever realized. Then, for my little sister—and for each of us as well—it would stand to reason (in a really reasonable way) that "I love you" must be stated; not just taken for granted through warm glances, flashing smiles, and occasional hugs. Lastly, I came to understand why each and every one of our *goodbyes* must be a "See you later!" She has always insisted on this. Perhaps truly seeing is a matter of the heart.

See you later, Alligator.

After while, Crocodile!

Chapter 15

Night Skies

"WHAT IS THE BEGINNING of eternity, the end of time and space, the beginning of every end, and the end of every place?" Daddy asked us. That took some pondering, and ended with him giving us the answer.[1]

"You must come outside, everyone, out here in the front yard," he announced one night. "Look up at that moon. This is the last time you will ever see our moon untouched by a human foot. Take a good look at it." We all went outside and we looked with him at the bright big moon, overhead. We gazed and we mused, and then we went back inside. What would become dawningly different here on our earth, with those footprints planted into the moon dust, in the year of 1969?

The best place for us to experience a night sky was the Bruneau Sand Dunes, which sat on the edge of the Owhyee dessert in the next valley to the west—Eagle Cove. We could sit around a congenial fire out in the open with family or with

---

[1]The answer to the riddle is the letter 'e.'

the "Young Peoples" group, roasting hot dogs and melting marshmallows for S'mores, while we gazed at the open night sky. The very best vantage point is atop one of the dunes, sitting together on its serpentine ridge. The embers from our fire below are the only terrestrial lights besides reflections from the Mountain Home Air Force Base, distant on the horizon horizon. That night sky was ours to enjoy, until it was time to go. And if a hay ride had taken us to the Dunes, well then we would star-gaze all the way back home.

Tall elm trees surrounded our yard at home, but a night slept out of doors, peeking at the patch of stars between the reach of the trees was a *must* for each summer. Out there, with a blanket pulled up under our chins, we would trace the Milky Way and catch any shooting stars we could, while swatting at any screeching mosquito circling our heads. We would excitedly locate the moving light of a satellite slowly and steadily traversing our planet.

"What's beyond the stars?" one of us would eventually begin.

— More stars.

— What's beyond more stars?

— More stars and more stars.

— What's beyond more stars and more stars?

— More stars, and more stars, and more stars.

— What's beyond more stars and more stars and more stars?

— More stars, and more stars, and more stars, and more stars.

— What's beyond...

Finally, the last of us was too sleepy to carry

the question any further into the yawning universe.

There was one place that was even better than the lawn, for a night sky. We had been building a hay stack out in an open field, spreading and placing with our hay forks the chopped alfalfa that Daddy dumped down from the farmhand tractor. Tomorrow the stack would be tall enough for its loaf-like top, all rounded so rain would roll off, and the hay kept dry for the cattle Daddy would winter over. The hay smelled so wholesomely sweet; I could imagine joining the cows for a breakfast on some nippy morning, for this cold cereal—milk poured on top. But, first we would sleep on it.

"Can we sleep on the hay stack, tonight, Mama?" Mama's 'yes' was conditioned on our ridding the blankets of hay stubble and any grass heads the next morning, and, of course, we would do that. We carried our blankets up the ladder leaning against the stack, and settled ourselves into custom-shaped depressions made into the soft hay. There the sky was opened up to us between the rimrocks and the southern desert horizon. Sheet lightening to the south might be part of the drama, or the distant red from a desert lightening fire. The next morning, when we pinned our blankets to the clothesline and dutifully pulled out the stubble and Cheatgrass, we didn't mind, for we had been star-blessed.

> *Cheatgrass, pay later*
> *Hand-picking barbs from blankets*
> *Worth a night's sleepout*

My brother Gary was a truly inventive Galileo. He used what he found to fashion a miniature telescope, and what he had found was a set of delightful small telescoping white cardboard tubes in the garbage. He glued lenses onto the tubes, and attached other telescope parts, including whittled wooden legs fastened with pin tips into the ends as a mount. I wasn't paying attention to his work, but Mama saw it finished and explained to him that his telescope was made from bathroom waste placed in the basket by one big sister, or the other. He maybe heard more than he bargained for, by way of explanation, but he understood why he should give his little telescope a coat of paint.

I came to need a vast sky filled with night-light wonder and unfathomable space mysteries, to hold the burgeoning universe of my developing adolescent brain. My, how the connections in my mind lit up, sparking new awareness, new understanding, even new wisdom, it seemed. "I should write these thoughts down!" I thought, amazed at such profundities. But alas, the insights came at random and inconvenient times for writing. And then they would be gone, temporary and fading flashes now out of reach, though leaving their trails and impressions behind them. *God is big and God is good*, I determined. And no matter how far my small bark might sail into the future and encounter unexpected gusts or currents, I would be okay.

Our valley of peaceful and surround-sound quiet grew us children up, secure and healthy. But it does take an over-aching vast vault of a night sky to nurture the imagination; to propel us beyond our little cove into the unknown and less certain waters, into a good life-long voyage.

Appendix I
Pigtails in Church

A

We hang our coats in the **anterooms**, the men and boys in the room to the left, and the women and girls to the right. Ours has a crib or two for the babies, and a little mirror hanging on the wall to check our hair, to put on our head coverings, or to give our cheeks a little pinching for blush.

I sing **alto** as soon as I catch on, and learn to read the shaped notes that go up and down on the lines in the church hymnal.

We sing **a capella**, all of our voices in four-part harmony filling the whole church clear up to its high ceiling.

B

Pastor Paul tells us in his sermons what the **bees** have taught him while out walking his ditch banks. I am surprised how God uses bees to talk to our preacher!

The **bishop** is Max Yoder. He comes over from Oregon to serve us communion, and to do baptisms and whatever else bishops do. Brother Yoder is a tall man with very big hands and a deep kind voice.

When I am **baptized**, water is poured into the bishop's hands and he opens them over my head. This is the pouring method. The warm water trickles through my hair and down my face, making my collar turn chilly wet against my neck. Lastly, his big hands turn over onto my head to give me a prayer blessing. Grown-ups shake my hand; I am now a member.

C

Now I wear the **covering** on my head, too. It is a stiff little cap made from see-through netting, shaped with crisp little darts. We hold our coverings in place with two long straight pins or bobby pins.

I take **communion**, eating the fresh little crackers Fan makes, and drinking the tiny glass of grape juice. We are remembering, like Jesus told us to do.

The **Charismatic Movement** was a big wind that blew across the country and swooped down on our own little congregation in the sixties. It made coverings fly off. It brought us **choruses** to sing and clap to, and for raising up our hands to God for worship.

D

We **draw** in church and make rubbings of coins or the harp design impressed into the front of the hymnal. A rubbing must be done as quietly as possible, stopping the pencil scratching while the preacher pauses.

E

Ernie is the only one exactly my age who grew all the way up in the Cove Church.

We have Children's Meeting in the **Evening Service**. We usually act out Bible stories for each other or hear about missionaries in far-off lands.

F

Communion includes a **foot washing**. We swap washing each other's feet in shiny tin buckets of warm water and dry them with white towels. The women and girls do it in the side room so we can unhook garters to take off our stockings.

Flannelgraph stories take us to Bible times.

On Sunday afternoons Mama shakes up a pan of hot buttered popcorn, and sometimes she stirs up a **fudge**, too.

G

The **Good** brothers are two dads who get their children's attention by snapping their fingers. They do this for their boys sitting on the back left bench with the other boys. Boys usually leave their marks carved into the back of the bench in front of them, using their fingernails to etch into the soft wood.

God's **grace** is something we especially hear a lot about from Pastor Amos. This means God is constantly giving us all the good things we don't deserve, like His great love.

H

The *Church Hymnal* and the *Life Songs* hold the **hymns** and songs we sing. Brother Leland is excellent at conducting us in a lively way with his right hand, while holding the songbook high in the other.

George **Hilty** is our oldest man in the church. He sits up in the front, always in the same place, sings tenor, and is the most devotional man I've seen. He often asks us to sing page 45 in the hymnal, *Lord, thou has searched and seen me through.* A set of teeth is one unnecessary thing for devoted singing.

Hiking is a great thing to do on a Sunday afternoon, maybe to the top of the rimrock, or out to the dump in the desert.

I

It is a good thing to grow up in the church in **Indian Cove**. The church is like a hub inside of the wheel of our Cove everyday-lives.

J

We learn all about **Jesus Christ**, who lived and died long ago to make us right with God. He especially loves children–*all the children of the world.*

We have **Junior Sewing Circle**. All junior girls meet and decorate quilt blocks with squeeze tube embroidery paints, or rip and roll bandages from old sheets for the lepers in Africa and India. We elect officers, hold meetings, and plan little parties. Our leader Edith Shenk only has boys in her family, so we figure she likes being with us girls, and we really like being with her.

K

We mostly use the **King James Version** of the Bible, which has the "thees" and "thous" in it. Some other versions come to church, too. Fan brings her *Amplified New Testament* and it helps to understand what God is saying to us.

L

The **Law** is about God's commandments that all of us, at one time and another, don't do right. This is why we need Jesus.

The really big decisions in the church were made by casting **lots**. Both men pick up a hymnal with a slip of paper in each. One of the papers will say, "You are chosen."

Lumber used to build our church house came from the Anderson Ranch Dam construction project up above Mountain Home. The men went up in trucks to collect it from the hillside and bring it down for our church. It was ready for our Sunday meetings in 1950—the year I was born.

M

We are a **Mennonite Church**, but then we changed the sign to just read, "Indian Cove Community Church," which is what we were, too.

God's **mercy** is when He doesn't give us what we really do deserve. Grace and mercy go together.

Barbara Miller is the Sunday School teacher who helps us to memorize verses the most. She gives us great little prizes when we do, like a glow-in-the-dark cross or miniature Bible story book.

N

We take quarters, **nickels**, dimes and pennies to Sunday School for God to use somewhere in the world. Daddy is the church treasurer, so we help him count out the offering on his flip-down desk at home. We stack up coins to make tens, fifties and hundreds for dollars.

O

There are no bathrooms in our church house, so we walk out to the **out-houses** when we need to go. One sits in the back right corner of the church yard for women and girls, and the other is out back on the left for the men and boys. I feel proud of our out-houses when visitors come and raise their eyebrows or whisper something while using one.

P

A church **potluck** is fun because we have more time to play and lots of good food. The mugs and bowls are all thick greenware, and the plates are heavy **pottery**.

We have a big **pulpit** with a cross on the front. My cousin Arden Kauffman made it in his shop class at school from pretty honey-colored wood.

We **polish** our shoes on Saturday night so they will be sitting ready for Sunday morning.

The song leader blows on the **pitch pipe** to show us what notes to begin singing on. Older girls and some of the grown-ups take turns leading the singing. It is fun to pick out the songs for Sunday morning, though I have to go to the bathroom a lot before I get my nerve up.

Q

Our Sunday School lessons are found in **Quarterlies** the church buys from Herald Press.

We all learn to sit **quietly** in church, no matter how young we are. We don't have to be as still and somber as we do when we play *Quakers Meeting.*[2]

The women have a Sewing Circle every month. Hear the clicking and the whirring of the treadle sewing machines as the ladies piece together the **quilts**. When we are wee ones, we play under the big stretched-out quilts and comforters while our mamas work overhead and talk the morning away together.

---

[2]This is how to play the "Quakers' Meeting" game: Gather children into a circle or on the steps. Everyone repeats together, "Quakers meeting has begun, no more talking, no more laughing shall be done." Then the one who is 'it' tries to make someone crack a smile, say something, giggle, or bust out laughing. Whoever does this becomes 'it.'

R

Cinnamon **rolls** or Cowboy Coffee Cake, with home-made cocoa poured over it, is our every Sunday breakfast.

After church we might have **rice** for dinner. The rice is warm, moist, and sweetened with cream and raisins, sprinkled with cinnamon. Or, dinner is a chicken or a beef **roast** pulled out of the oven as soon as we get home, surrounded with our own good garden vegetables.

Reading and writing letters are some ways to take a rest on Sundays. **Resting** from work, except for the necessary farm chores and the dishes, is a good thing for all. Some of our neighbors do their resting on Saturdays.

S

I remember how good it is when I just know God's Holy **Spirit** is with us, teaching us, and leading our church service when we let Him.

Once in awhile, we have a **Singsperation.** Then it is all singing and no sermon. Anyone can make a special request for a song.

Here are some things to **see** and ponder at church: If we stare at the back of Brother Snider's head long enough will he reach up and scratch it? Lay back against the bench and count the squares in the ceiling tiles overhead. Do you think that shining spot on Pastor Amos' forehead means he might be anointed?

T

We play **tag** around the cars after church. This is best done at nighttime when it's dark and scary outside.

A **testimony** is when someone tells about what God is doing in their life. This can be interesting stuff.

U

A song to sing on Easter Sunday is **Up From the Grave He Arose**, page 284 in the Hymnal. The notes rise up and up on the page and so do our voices.

V

The Bible is divided into **verses**, which makes it easier to read since there are many stopping places to pick from.

In June, the church has a **Vacation Bible School** for all of us children. Fan is the best storyteller of all time! You would agree if *you* could see and hear her.

W

Once a year, our church gets together with the other Mennonites from Nampa and Filer for a **"Workers' Meeting."** There are lots of talks and lots of singing. We get our annual kick out of singing page #112 in the Life Songs with Junior Miller from Filer leading us.

The **windows** of the church house are all along the west side, and are made of a glass we can't see out, unless they are cranked open. When the sun is going down, the evening light streams through the glass while we sing, *Day is dying in the west; Heaven is touching earth with rest...* This restfulness gets us all ready to go straight to bed when we get home.

X

We make **X's and O's** in the notes we write to each other. Each X means a kiss and each O is a hug. You can use as many as you wish, depending on who the note is for.

Y

We look forward to **"Young People's,"** once we've become teens. There are wiener roasts, hay rides, exciting games like "Walk-a-Mile," camping up at Bennett Mountain, making root beer, and any other fun things we come up with.

Z

We fall asleep on the benches when we are little. A very good time to fall asleep is on the way home in the car, so Daddy will carry us into the house to our beds. **ZZZzzzzzz...**

Sunday Breakfast

Saturday was baking day, and that could mean a batch of cinnamon rolls or maple bars for breakfast the next day. If not, Sunday mornings have just enough time before going to church for mixing up a coffee cake to serve with our standard cups of hot cocoa. Sunday breakfast was part of what made Sunday special, along with a squeaky-clean house.

Cowboy Coffee Cake

¼ cup butter
⅔ cup brown sugar
1 egg
1½ cups flour
3 tsp. baking powder
¼ tsp. salt
½ cup milk

Combine and mix the first three ingredients. Mix together the flour, baking powder, and salt, and add to mixture along with the milk. Batter should be soft like cake batter. If not, add more milk or water. Pour into greased square or round pan. Put topping over batter.

Topping: Mix together ½ cup brown sugar, ¼ cup butter, ¼ cup flour, 1 tsp. cinnamon.

Bake 350 °F for 25-30 minutes. Serve with hot cocoa.

Mom's Maple Bars

½ cup butter
½ cup sugar
2 eggs, beaten
1 tsp. salt
2 T. yeast
2 cups warm water
8 cups flour

Dissolve yeast in the warm water. Mix butter, sugar, eggs, and salt. Combine with yeast. Gradually add in flour, and knead. Set aside to raise until doubled. Punch down.

Roll out to ¼ inch thickness and cut into rectangular bars. Let bars raise on a floured surface for 1 hour. Fry in oil preheated to 375 °F. Drain on rack or absorbent paper. Allow to partly cool. Spread with Maple Glaze (recipe on following page). Serve warm with hot cocoa.

Maple Bar Glaze

¾ cup butter
½ cup milk
½ cup sugar
Powdered sugar
1 tsp. Mapleine or Maple extract

Combine milk, sugar, and butter in saucepan and cook until dissolved. Add enough powdered sugar to the hot mixture to be spreadable. Beat together and add the amount of maple flavoring you like. Spread on bars while hot, for a smooth and glossy glaze.

Appendix II
Photo Album

Baby Maxine with Daddy & Judy in Sunday best,
sitting on the cellar steps.

Judy makes shadow profiles in the Mercury's hubcap while Daddy takes a picture of his little family in 1951.

Indian Cove Mennonite Church.

Neighbor Dave gave us girls leather chaps to wear for bucking straw bales.

Grandpa Shank helping us stack chopped hay. The hay stack will grow 20—22 feet high, nicely rounded on top, like a loaf of bread.

We are proud of Daddy's prize-winning sugar
beets!

Mrs. Thompson's 5th grade class.

Mrs. Thompson's 6th grade class.

I LOVE IDAHO'S INDIAN COVE !

I've reached the land of corn and hay,
Of cattle, sheep and honey sweet.
I got my farm through F.H.A.
And now I'm busy night and day.

Chorus-
Oh Idaho, Sweet Indian Cove!
As on the highest rim I rove-
I look away across my field
And wonder what my crops will yield.
And then I view my crop of hay.
And now I know I'm doomed to stay.

2   I hear the howl the coyote makes,
The charming of the rattle snakes.
Of all the sores the sand-burrs make
Be careful Son, for piy's sake!

3   I love my home in Idaho
Where fragrant sagebrush chose to grow;
Where peaceful rimrocks steeply rise-
To praise the MAKER of the skies.

Final Chorus-
Oh Idaho. Sweet Indian Cove!
As on the highest rim I rove-
The lightning flashes. Thunder rolls.
The wind blows wild! But God controls.
I see Snake River's winding trails.
I know that here God's LOVE prevails.

                    --- Composed by- O. W. King
                        Final Chorus by- Betty Kauffman

To be sung to the tune of- Beulah Land.

Recipe Index

Made in the USA
San Bernardino, CA
19 January 2019